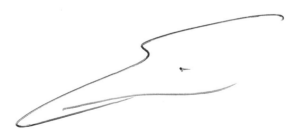

"It is the complexities of life coupled with two cultures that make this a powerful story. This memoir takes you on a journey involving sacrifice, sadness, hard work, happiness, and inner peace."

— **Stephan Passalacqua**, Lawyer

"Most of us are eager to produce a long list of mostly valid reasons pointing to why something cannot or should not be done. The successful among us simply do it. The impossible is achieved every day, albeit not without difficulty. This is the remarkable true story of one woman's journey between two vastly different parallel worlds. It is the jaw-dropping, determined pursuit of a life that should have been out of her reach. This book will cause anyone to re-think the words *I can't*."

— **Mike Masi**, Author of *A Day That God Made*

Goodbye Istanbul

Goodbye Istanbul

EMINE LOXLEY

How a Young Girl
from the Middle East
Discovered the
American Dream

HIGH-FIVE PRESS

Goodbye Istanbul

*How a Young Girl from the Middle East Discovered
the American Dream*

Emine Loxley

ISBN: 978-1-942545-58-3

Library of Congress Control Number: 2016911142

HIGH-FIVE PRESS

Published by High-Five Press

An imprint of Wyatt-MacKenzie

DEDICATION

To my family.

TABLE OF CONTENTS

PROLOGUE · iii

CHAPTER ONE · 1
A Child No Longer

CHAPTER TWO · 15
Beckoning to Me

CHAPTER THREE · 27
"Come to the States"

CHAPTER FOUR · 37
From Sea to Shining Sea

CHAPTER FIVE · 45
Man and Wife

CHAPTER SIX · 57
Citizen

CHAPTER SEVEN · 67
Pre-med and Potatoes

CHAPTER EIGHT · 77
Captain

CHAPTER NINE · 93
Proud

CHAPTER TEN · 105
Leaving

CHAPTER ELEVEN · 113
Bend

CHAPTER TWELVE · 127
Willem

CHAPTER THIRTEEN · 141
The Dream

MY MOTHER TELLS THE STORY and I am reluctant to believe it. Not because I don't believe my mother, but because such a story simply cannot be true. In the end, I decide it happened just as my mother says. It was Turkey in the early 1960s, after all. It was the culture of the country, indeed the culture of the Middle East. Then again, the story could be present day. What has changed?

My grandfather, the story goes, was riding on a tractor with a man. My mother, all of thirteen, was walking nearby, on her way to get some water for the household, wearing a skirt but no pants underneath the skirt, as was required by religious custom. It was summer; it was achingly hot. But the transgression allowed the lower portion of my mother's legs to be visible. The driver of the tractor noticed, and, momentarily distracted, ran the tractor into a short retaining wall. My grandfather was furious. At my mother.

He jumped down from the tractor and grabbed his daughter by the arm and led her across the field to their house where he picked her up under her arms and sat her down harshly on a table.

"If you insist on showing your legs," he declared, "then we will have to remove the offending legs." With that, he grabbed an axe while my mother screamed in horror.

My uncle, my mother's older brother, had witnessed the incident and came running into the house. Knowing he would not have been able to reason with his father about the propriety or impropriety of a thirteen-year-old girl wearing a skirt with no pants on a hot summer day, he tried a different tack.

"Father," he said, "forget this for now. You've been working hard and it is time to take a break. Let's go have tea and then we can come back later and deal with this."

My grandfather put down the axe and accepted his son's invitation and nothing more was ever said about the episode. Would he have used the axe had my uncle not come into the house? Who can say? My mother thinks yes. I have to believe no. But the image of a father threatening with impunity his daughter with an axe is disturbing enough.

And my grandfather's response didn't stop there. If he didn't chop his daughter's legs off that day in a literal sense, he was soon to take them out from under her in a figurative, symbolic sense. She was old enough to elicit interest from men and she could not, therefore, be allowed to remain single and unattached. My grandfather would not risk having the town think of his daughter as a whore. A marriage was quickly arranged. At thirteen, my mother became the wife of an eighteen-year-old boy whom she didn't even know.

I grew up in the same culture. I wore pants under my skirt. I acted in accordance with the prevailing customs. I was destined for a life not unlike the life of my mother – housewife and subordinate to her husband. But by the time I was thirteen, the age of my mother when she'd been forced to marry, I'd made up my mind: my life would be different. I didn't know exactly what it would take or how I was going to manage it, but I would find a way to get out. I would find a way to escape – the country, the culture, the prearranged destiny of a Middle Eastern woman. My life, I decided by the age of thirteen, was going to be markedly different.

CHAPTER ONE

A Child No Longer

AS A YOUNG MAN OF EIGHTEEN, my father had his eyes on a girl in the village in which he was raised, a small village in the Turkish province of Çorum. But my father's parents were introduced to a couple from another village who were looking for a suitable husband for their thirteen-year-old daughter. She was attracting the attention of men and therefore it was time for her to become somebody's wife. The couples hit it off and it was decided that their children would be married. My father would have to forget the girl from his village.

My parents met for the first time at their own engagement party. Traditional Turkish engagement parties are celebratory affairs not unlike Western weddings. Relatives and neighbors and friends all come. There is a bounty of food served and blessings are offered. The engagement rings, tied together with a red ribbon, are brought forth on a special presentation tray. Cake is eaten. It's a happy time for the families. The celebration of something new. For the bride and groom in such arranged circumstances it is more of a duty, a commitment to tradition. A commitment that lasts a lifetime.

My mother would tell me of the relief she felt when she saw her husband-to-be for the first time. She had often imagined the worst. But there were no physical deformities, no unsightly features. In fact he was not unattractive and he was also not without charm. My father felt the same relief, although it no doubt had to have been clouded by the feelings he'd had for the girl back in his own village.

I was born two years later when my mother was fifteen, more than old enough by Turkish standards to have a child. My father's older brother helped take care of me for a short time while my father spent time away, first during his mandatory military service, and then trying to find work. My mother knew next to nothing about taking care of a baby. In time, of course, she would learn, and when my father returned to the household, my parents had another girl – my sister Naime.

But there was little for my father to do in the village and before I was three, we would move out of the province of Çorum to the big city of Istanbul, four-hundred miles to the west. There would be more opportunities for work for a young man in the city. But there was another reason for the move besides work. My grandfather sensed that my father still had a romantic interest in the girl from the village and he reckoned that so long as that interest was alive, my father could never focus completely on his family. And so the move was made more or less at my grandfather's insistence. My father would never see the girl again.

Istanbul straddles the Bosphorus strait that runs between the Black Sea and the Sea of Marmara, and thus it straddles two continents. Along the water and towards the western part of the city, resting at the doorstep of Europe, is the commercial center of Istanbul, along with the historical and cultural sections of the city. This is where the tourists go. This is the part you see in movies. There is the energy of a world-class city with hotels and cafés and nightlife. There are lively bazaars and there is beautiful architecture and a skyline marked by minarets and historic mosques.

We lived in the rural outskirts, the city center being much too costly for us. We didn't see many tourists. Our part of Istanbul was mostly small family farms – there were cows and chickens and goats and sheep, and grape vines and fields of corn that I would run through and hide in as a child. Our tiny house had been slapped together in a few days by my father and his younger brother who had come to Istanbul from Ankara to help us get settled. It was four walls and a sagging roof. It was all my father could afford. Years later, after I would leave Turkey, the city would deem the house unsafe and it had to be torn down and rebuilt – this time with the proper permits and by licensed contractors, neither of which were common back in the days I was growing up there.

Unlike in the heart of the city, there was little modernization in our neighborhood. Our house had no electricity and no running water, but of course as a small child, I assumed this was the way the whole world lived. I would be sent a half mile to retrieve water, filling up two wooden buckets that would hang, one on each end, to a pole that I would carry across my back. It was hard work for a child and more often than not, by the time I'd get home after struggling with my load as it sloshed around with each unsteady step, at least half the water would have been spilled out of the buckets.

When I was in high school, we would finally

get electricity to our house, a single wire that ran from the main line along the street. It seemed like magic to me. But we would disconnect it during the day for fear of running up the bill, utilizing it only when we needed light. Until then, through elementary and middle school, I did my homework by the light of an oil lamp.

My father, an uneducated man who could neither read nor write, found work where he could – at the farmer's market, or working small construction jobs, often pouring and carrying concrete from which the houses in Turkey were all made. On weekends, beginning when I was just seven, I would help him at the job sites. You were never too young to work and bring money into the household.

Eventually, my father took a position working in the laundry of the local children's hospital, still working side jobs to help make ends meet. When I became a little older, I was embarrassed by the laundry position. It was menial work. Other kids had fathers who were physicians at the hospital, not laundry workers. I never told anybody – classmates at school, for instance – exactly what my father did for a living. When I became older still, I gained more of an appreciation for my father for his work in the hospital for I understood the reason behind it. Without his employment there, we would never have been able to secure the level of healthcare that we received for Riza.

Riza was born a few years after Naime, a healthy baby boy. But around the age of three, he suddenly developed problems with his feet and legs. He had difficulty walking. I remember a doctor trying to tickle the bottoms of Riza's feet for a reaction that didn't come. My brother was diagnosed with polio. My mother was religious in a mainstream Islamic way, but she was also superstitious and given to a mixture of supernatural beliefs. If Riza was afflicted with some kind of disease, it most likely was the result of evil spirits – ghosts that had to be exorcized, something that not even the best medical doctors could do. And so my mother went to a variety of spiritual healers and imams, each one promising hope, none of them delivering it. I was young, but I knew even then that my mother was wasting her time, not to mention hard-earned money.

Hope eventually came with the contacts that my father would make at the hospital – the doctors and nurses who knew him and were able to help us shortcut the nation's socialized medical system and give Riza a little extra attention and in a shorter period of time. The people at the hospital liked my father and they went out of their way to help. Riza would soon be fitted with special shoes and leg braces. He could walk, although it would be with difficulty. When it rained, the mile-long dirt road that we would traverse each day to get to school would become mud, and besides the added struggle for Riza, there was the nuisance of the metal braces getting wet, caked with mud and hard to clean, and prone to rust. At these times my mother would carry Riza on her back to and from school, slogging through the mud herself. Each and every time she did this, until Riza eventually became too big for her to carry.

After Riza came my youngest brother Murat. And so our parents had two girls and two boys. Our childhoods were happy ones for the most part. In the neighborhood, there were lots of kids and we would play soccer or jump rope or climb the many fig trees. We'd hike and pick berries or pilfer walnuts from somebody's grove of walnut trees, sometimes getting chased off of their property.

My parents provided a safe and secure home environment and though their marriage was based on a commitment others had forced upon them, somehow the marriage worked. Each was comfortable with the other. There was a clear delineation of responsibilities and I can remember exactly one instance when my parents disagreed, though I can no longer remember about what. Of course in keeping with Turkish culture, my father had the last word on any subject, but my mother was not without influence. My father worked, supported the family, and outwardly was in charge. But in reality, we all knew, my father included, that the household was run by my mother.

My mother, notwithstanding her penchant for superstition and dependence on spiritual healers, was logical and steady and strong. Our backbone. She was intelligent and I wonder often at how far she could have gone with an education, and in a different culture. She was a plain-looking woman, even stern. And always serious; I can't remember a single time that I caught her laughing. My father, on the other hand, was more jovial, more fun, more emotional. He was lean but strong, handsome with a swarthy complexion and the rugged facial features of Middle Eastern men. He had a mustache and a smile that would be reflected by a twinkle in his eyes. Between my parents and their children, there was little demonstrative affection. Between my parents themselves, there was none. It was a functional family marked not so much by love as by respect – for each other, for the value of family, and for the traditions of the culture.

In school, we learned all about Mustafa Kemal, a military commander in World War I who distinguished himself in the Battle of Gallipoli against the invading Anzacs. Later, he would earn the surname *Atatürk*, "Father of the Turks." In the aftermath of the war and the wreckage of the Ottoman Empire, he led Turkey in its war of independence from the occupying forces, becoming the first president of the modern-day nation. He was our George Washington. Later, after I left Turkey, I learned more about Atatürk's authoritarian, dictatorial, even brutal ways. I learned things you couldn't learn in Turkey, at least not in grade school.

We were taught Islam in school, as well, but little of it would resonate with me. In seventh grade, the teacher was lecturing us about God and creation, and I asked about something I was genuinely curious about. "If you look at an apple," I said, "it might look beautiful. That's a creation of God, isn't it? But if you cut the apple open, suppose there's a worm inside. Would God have put that worm there? And why?" I guess I was asking a larger metaphysical question about the role of God in the universe, and perhaps nature's role. Or maybe it was a question about the imperfections of God's creation. I wasn't old enough to understand the depth of my own query, but I should have been old enough to know that you don't question God's creation in a Turkish classroom. I didn't get a satisfactory answer. I didn't get an answer at all. The teacher wasn't interested in discussing theological subtleties and, in fact, ultimately refused to give me a passing grade in the class which meant I couldn't graduate from the school. My parents would have to enroll me in another school, giving me strict instructions not to question the teachers this time around.

It wasn't my first brush-up against Islam. Between fifth and sixth grade, there was a summer school at a local mosque that my mother sent us kids to where we were to learn Arabic and the Koran. We were required to sit quietly on the floor, cross-legged, our feet under our legs. My foot began to fall asleep and I instinctively stretched it out in front of me, an offense to the requisite decorum, and I was slapped hard on the head by the imam. That night I told my mother I didn't want to go back to the mosque. "Then you don't have to go," she said. She may have been a believer, but she was never forceful about her beliefs, never demanded that her children toe any hard and fast theological line. I was encouraged by my mother to think for myself and I would eventually come to understand that the encouragement came because my mother had been restricted by a culture that largely would not allow her to do so.

That understanding had become clear to me towards the end of elementary school. I had been passed from grade to grade. But I could barely read or write. It was a small school and I had the same teacher for grades one through five. Compared to some of the other kids in the classroom, smarter kids from wealthier families, kids with better opportunities to someday further their education at a university, I was not worth the teacher's time or energy. There was no future for me academically. The teacher kept passing me along, figuring I was only going to be a housewife anyway. I had no reason to learn to read or write. I would serve a husband, most likely in an arranged marriage to a man my father would find for me.

In actuality, I was not unintelligent. I was simply not a good student and I was not a motivated one. I was a daydreamer who had trouble focusing. My body was in the classroom but my mind was on the other side of the window that I could not stop looking out of. Mentally, I was climbing fig trees and running through the cornfields. All I wanted was for class to be over so I could jump rope or pick berries. Although I might have been a curious child, learning about the world outside of my neighborhood in Istanbul was not a high priority. I had no understanding of what an education could do for me (or what a lack of education could stop me from doing).

All that changed for me in fifth grade after a conference my teacher had with my mother. It was just a standard parent-teacher conference, meaning very little to the teacher. For my mother, however, it was the first time she was made to understand my ineptitude as a student. For the teacher, I imagine the conference was just a means by which to confirm for my mother what she probably assumed my mother had already known: a future of opportunity that included a university education was not in the cards for me. But I could certainly be a fine housewife and mother.

As it happened, my mother had not known this and the realization disturbed her greatly. In me, she had seen the chance for a better life than her own. She had seen a future the teacher hadn't. She took me aside and spoke to me as she had never spoken before.

"Emi," she said. "Don't you see? Don't you see what will happen to you if you don't work harder at your schoolwork? You're a smart girl. I know this. If you take school seriously and study and learn, you can go anywhere. You can go to the university. You can make something of your life. You have to work harder, Emi." The idea of making something of my life had never really occurred to me before then. My future wasn't anything I had ever thought about.

My mother continued: "If you don't, do you know what will happen? Do you? Your father will find you a husband. Very soon, Emi. You will end up...you will end up like me. Look around you, Emi." She waved her arms around her, taking in the entirety of our small home. "Is this what you want? Your life will be a house like this one. You will cook for your family and clean for them. That will be your life, Emi. When your husband comes home at the end of the day, you will heat up the water so that you can wash his feet and hands. You will make dinner for him, and for your children. That's what you will do. That will be *all* that you will do. This. This will be your life."

Then she walked out of the room, leaving me alone with my thoughts. I might not have realized the import of the moment at the time, but something changed in me just then. It was as if a light had been turned on. For the very first time, I began thinking about my future. I might have only been in fifth grade, just a twelve-year-old girl, but I was suddenly a child no longer.

CHAPTER TWO

Beckoning to Me

AFTER MY MOTHER'S TALK, I focused completely on my studies. I worked hard. I paid attention in class. I don't ever remember playing again, climbing fig trees, running through cornfields. I studied nonstop, catching up to my classmates and eventually even surpassing them, getting A's in all my classes except, of course, for the religion class in seventh grade when I questioned the teacher about God and creation.

But being a good student didn't necessarily mean I was always obedient, at least around the house. I'd become savvy enough to stop questioning my teachers, but I didn't stop questioning my parents. My parents, being uneducated, respected anyone with an education. We argued once about someone we had heard about who had been arrested for no apparent cause. "The police have too much power," I said.

"Emi!" my father said, "how can you say

such a thing? The police are all very well-schooled and trained. They know what they are doing."

"But that doesn't make them honest!" I countered.

"You should not say such things," he said, shaking his head disapprovingly. "You should not say such things!"

"Why not? Will they throw me in jail, too? Can I not have an opinion?"

"Emi!"

The world of my parents, like the world of many people growing up in Turkey back in those days, and even today for many Middle Eastern families, was a closed one. They couldn't read or write and until we finally got a television set, any ideas about the outside world came almost entirely through the small radio that sat in our living room.

For me, a big part of the problem was my gender. It was one thing for a man to express an opinion, quite another for a woman. In high school the American comedy film *Private Benjamin* came out. Goldie Hawn played an army recruit and we all watched the movie. At a family gathering one Sunday the men were discussing it along with the absurdity of having a woman in the army.

"Why can't a woman be in the army?" I said.

"Women would be bad fighters," my uncle said.

"And they're not smart enough," another uncle said.

"A woman can be every bit as smart as a man!" I declared, to which they all just laughed.

My outspokenness was especially troubling for my mother. "No Turkish man is going to want to marry you, Emi," she would say. "You are too opinionated. Too brazen."

"Just as well," I would answer. "I don't want to marry a Turkish man, anyway. I don't want my whole life to be serving a man. I don't want to be tied down." I didn't stop, of course, to think of how my mother might have taken this. It was her idea, of course, that I "make something of myself" but that didn't mean turning my back on convention. Her idea was for me to get an education, maybe go to the university. Perhaps even have a career. But my duties as someone's wife would always come first. I could better myself, make some money, marry whom I wanted – but all within the confines of traditional Turkish culture.

In addition to studying hard in school, I worked. During one summer, Naime and I took jobs with a family who did contract work for a clothing manufacturer. It was common for households to work in such a way, doing piecemeal work for local factories. There were four employees – all school children (there were no child labor laws) – and we worked in assembly-line fashion, piecing together material to be finished into socks. We would sew together the toe parts of the socks and then iron them and clip the socks together and package them in plastic bags.

When I got into high school, I worked summers in a larger textile operation, cutting fabric from patterns into sleeves or pant legs, which I would then turn over to the people who ran the industrial sewing machines. The textile industry was a huge part of the Turkish economy and kids were always sought after to take the low-paying manual jobs. My income went to the household. It was an unspoken expectation of my parents. My money was the family's money. My father made enough for us to live on, but my income helped with the extras. We could eat a little better, for instance, and seeing the fruits (sometimes literally) of my work made an important early impression on me: hard work had its rewards.

By then, the outside world was beginning to find me, or maybe I was just starting to pay more attention to outside influences. In particular, there were the Turkish families that had returned from labor work in Germany. From the mid 1950s through the early '70s, West Germany recruited millions of guest workers to help with the rebuilding of their country following the devastation of World War II. The workers came from Italy first, but then from countries farther away, mostly third-world countries where labor could be hired cheaply. In time, the majority of the laborers would be Turkish.

Many stayed in Germany and today Turks comprise Germany's largest ethnic minority. But many returned, coming back much wealthier, by Turkish standards, than when they had left. My father at one time had wanted to move to Germany for the work, but due to a problem with his hearing, he was unable to pass the necessary physical. It was greatly disappointing for him, made worse by the returning families who wore better clothes and lived in bigger houses. It was probably my father's biggest regret that he could not take his family to Germany for a better life.

I saw the better clothes and the bigger houses, too, and I made up my mind that, someday, I would leave Turkey. I would go to Germany to live. If not Germany, certainly somewhere in Europe. Perhaps England. Western-style culture began to beckon to me. It seemed to me that there were places in the world where you had the opportunity to greatly improve your lot in life if you were willing to put in the work. Though Turkey was more or less aligned with the West during the Cold War, there was still a widely held belief that communism was a more "fair" and more "equitable" way of life. Everybody could have a house. Everybody could eat well. Everybody could have access to a doctor. Nobody would take more than anybody else. To a population of poor people, this was an attractive idea. Everywhere, it seemed to me, including in school, Western capitalism was always presented as callous and unjust, propelled entirely by greed. The United States in particular was always being denigrated; Americans were materialistic and self-indulgent. But I liked the idea that you could become something better than what you were. With capitalism, you could dream big and if you worked hard, your dreams could come true. To me, it just seemed like communism was a way for everybody to be equally poor.

My high school was in the city. There were schools closer to our house, but the high school I chose to attend was more of a vocational-technical type school that centered its curriculum on the textile trade. My major interest was design. Our school days would be split between a half day of regular education and a half day of training for our future jobs. I liked the school and I liked the idea of getting away from home for the day and going into the city.

Not far from the high school was the world-famous Grand Bazaar. Istanbul's Grand Bazaar is one of the oldest and biggest in the world, with over three-thousand shops that attract hundreds of thousands of people every day. I loved the energy of the place. To earn more money, I went to work in a shop at the Grand Bazaar on Saturdays. The shop sold jewelry and rugs and I would model the jewelry for the customers – putting on earrings or necklaces. I made an agreement with the shop owner to be paid in dollars instead of Turkish liras. And I began hanging on to my wages, sharing less of my earnings with the household. What I gave to my father was sufficient. I hid the rest in my room, eventually buying gold with it and saving it for my eventual exit from Turkey.

Since the great majority of the shoppers at the Bazaar were tourists, I began to meet a lot of people from all over the world, including the United States. It was my first real interaction with Americans and I decided I liked them. They didn't seem self-indulgent to me; they seemed friendly and outgoing. Spending my Saturdays in an environment where most of the people were from elsewhere opened up my eyes even more to the outside world. Many of the tourists were young and seemed educated and prosperous, and wore nice clothes. They were more sophisticated than the people I had known. The city itself was more cosmopolitan, at least as compared with our neighborhood on the outskirts of town. It was vibrant and alive and the people always seemed like they had places to go.

I noticed the attractive clothes of the women tourists and I imagined wearing the same clothes. In European glamour magazines, too, I saw women with beautiful hair and fashionable attire and I wondered why I had to cover myself up. Why couldn't I wear a short skirt or have my hair done or paint my nails? Why couldn't I dress like the women in the magazines? I began wearing jeans (without a skirt over top) – a small start towards more stylish fashion – but my father protested. Fortunately, my uncles – my mother's brothers – who were both in universities, talked with my father and informed him that in the city, it was okay for a woman to wear jeans. "It's different than it is out here," my one uncle told him. "It's okay. Emi is fine. Leave her alone." My father listened to my uncles. They were not only educated, but they were from the same province of Çorum that he was from, from the same small village as my mother. He respected their backgrounds and he respected their education.

That a person from a poor village could even get into the university was remarkable. That two people from the same family could do so was practically unheard of. But both my uncles were very smart and both passed their entrance exams on the first try. This was no small thing: in those days, you only were given one try. One uncle enrolled in Marmara University in Istanbul, the other in Ankara University. Both did exceptionally well. My mother, of course, had the same smart genes as her brothers and I often thought she may have possessed even more raw intelligence. But there could be no university for a poor village girl.

I, too, respected my uncles. They lived in dormitories in their own rooms, which I found greatly intriguing. As a girl, in our neighborhood, you lived with your parents until you married at which point you lived with your husband. Even if I had been allowed to leave the house and rent a flat somewhere, there would have been no one who would have rented me one. It would have bordered on scandalous. No single girl lived by herself.

Meanwhile, work and school were both taking me further into the textile trade. Later in life, I would come to the realization that my opportunity to develop an actual career was helped enormously by the fact that I was the oldest of my parents' children. Had I an older sibling – particularly an older brother – my path would not have been much different than the path of my mother. It would have been the older brother who would have gotten a job to help with the family finances. It would have been the older brother who would have acquired the high school education (maybe even gone on to the university) to help my parents who could neither read nor write. My older brother would have taken those responsibilities. It would have been his role as the eldest sibling. I would have been taught other things – how to cook, how to clean. I would have been taught how to be a good wife.

In my last year of high school, I secured an internship position with a textile factory, part of a larger international company with an office in New York. It was an unpaid internship but I worked as hard as if they were paying me the salary of an executive. I wanted to make an impression. I arrived early each day and stayed late. Even though my specialty was design, as interns we had to learn every facet of the business. I learned everything I could about the manufacturing machines. The machine vendor reps would come and give training sessions for the employees on how to operate the machines and troubleshoot problems. I soaked up everything, impressing the reps with my willingness to learn. They'd often mention me to the owner of the factory. "Keep an eye on that one," they'd say.

In the design section, we'd often have to deal with vendors of fabric, many of whom would come from Europe. But the language of choice between the vendors and the company employees was English. We had translators on hand for those of us who couldn't understand the English being spoken and before long it occurred to me that it would be a huge advantage for me to learn English. Two nights a week, I began to take English language classes. The idea was to help advance me in my career, open up some opportunities, maybe somehow provide me with a way out of Turkey. I was still thinking Germany. This was February of 1984. How could I have known then that by June of that year, I'd not only be out of Turkey, I'd be living in the United States of America?

CHAPTER THREE

"Come to the States"

TRAVELING AWAY FROM HOME, although a dream of mine, was something I was altogether unfamiliar with. Throughout my childhood, it could only be a dream and nothing more. My parents were too poor to take us anywhere. There was no such thing as a vacation. My only real time away from home was when I was twelve and my parents sent me to live with my grandmother back in Çorum for the summer. My grandmother's little village was even more rural than our neighborhood outside of Istanbul. I missed home. I missed my sister and brothers. When it was finally time to go back to Istanbul, I cried because my aunt in Çorum had donkeys and there was a particular baby donkey that I wanted to take back with me. My aunt wouldn't allow it.

But travel started becoming more realistic for me by the end of high school, mainly because I was meeting foreigners and hearing about other parts of the world. The concept of going else-where seemed much less abstract. At the Bazaar, I met four American soldiers who were stationed at a U.S. Army base called Çakmaklı, not too far outside of Istanbul. They would come into the Bazaar regularly, buying things for their families back in the States, sending rugs back home and other Turkish souvenirs. They brought an inter-preter friend with them named Hakan and through Hakan we would always talk and in time we became good friends. The soldiers lived to-gether off base in a high-end apartment, part of a complex called Yeşil Köy ("Green Village") which sat right on the beach. I assumed the soldiers must have been wealthy. Only later would I learn (firsthand) that American soldiers don't make a lot of money. Yeşil Köy might have been exclusive by Turkish standards, but it didn't require a lot of wealth for four people to split the rent with American dollars.

Every weekend the soldiers would come to the Bazaar and soon they were asking me to come along with them to listen to music somewhere or to just hang out with them. It was fun to be with them and it was enlightening to hear about their time and travels in the military. I was still just learning the very basics of English so Hakan was kept busy as my friendship with the soldiers grew. I told them of my desire to someday leave Turkey, become fluent in English, see other parts of the world.

"Come to the States," one of them said.

"But how can I afford it?" I replied. "I have the money to get there, but I wouldn't be able to afford to stay. How would I support myself? How could I get a job?"

"Well, you can be my baby's nanny," said Joel, the oldest of the soldiers. He was married and his wife and baby lived in upstate New York, wherever that was.

"Really?"

"Sure," he said. "I mean, why not?"

Over the course of several weeks, he made the offer more than a couple of times, always in a sort of offhand way that I was too unschooled in English to recognize as flippant. In retrospect, it was easy to see that his offer was just one of those things that someone might say to be nice. A pretense of generosity. He couldn't have imagined that I might accept it. In truth, Joel no doubt knew of the difficulty I'd have getting a visa. You had to prove you had a valid reason for traveling out of the country – work, perhaps, or maybe to visit an ill relative – and you had to prove you were coming back again. And for all Joel knew, my spoken desires to travel were just the dreams of a poor, naive Turkish girl with an overactive imagination. It was a seemingly harmless offer that most likely nothing would come of.

And I *was* naive. Naive enough to assume Joel was sincere. I approached my boss at the textile factory – Mr. Aykaç, a short, older man with white hair. He had always been especially nice to me and I was hopeful he could help me secure a visa. My travel to the States wouldn't exactly be work-related, of course. Still, immersing myself in American culture would certainly help me learn English faster which, I explained to Mr. Aykaç, could be of enormous benefit at the factory for dealing with the foreign vendors and customers that we dealt with every day. It could make me a more valuable employee. But Mr. Aykaç knew that my asking was more or less as a personal favor.

"Have you ever been outside of Istanbul?" he asked.

"No."

"If you go over there, Emine, you won't come back."

"Of course I will."

"I don't think so."

"Give me six months, Mr. Aykaç. If I don't come back, there are plenty of other students who can replace me as an intern for you here. I'll give you the name of a classmate who would fit in perfectly."

In fact, there was a small part of me that imagined staying permanently in America once I got there. But practically speaking, I knew there was little chance of that happening. Unless I married an American man or could somehow get a job that would allow for a permanent work visa or secure a scholarship so that I could get a student visa, I was sure to be ultimately deported. And none of those things were realistic. It could only be a temporary stay, but temporary was better than nothing.

The funny thing is, I didn't even know anything about America. Not really. When I was in high school, my family finally bought a television set. It was a small black and white model and we would watch reruns, dubbed in Turkish, of American shows like "Dallas," "The Waltons," and "Little House on the Prairie." From these, I cobbled together a rudimentary view of America. "Little House on the Prairie" gave me an idea as to the cultural background of the country while "The Waltons" and "Dallas" competed to educate me on American values. John-Boy versus J.R. Ewing. Eventually, I came to believe that because "Dallas" was more contemporary, and because it was soon followed up with the similarly-themed "Dynasty,"

Americans were all just simply rich and powerful, albeit a bit scheming and manipulative.

But my first interaction with real Americans was at the Bazaar and my friendships with the soldiers ultimately gave me a very positive impression of the United States. Whether I could stay or not, or even if I would ever be able to return to the States afterwards, I just wanted to see America, live like an American for whatever period of time I could. If nothing else, I knew my command of the English language would greatly improve.

Mr. Aykaç was good enough to agree to help me get a visa, even if he remained doubtful about my eventual return. He wrote a letter which was signed off on by all the departments at the factory – dye, design, and thread – and I took it to the consulate which provided me with an indefinite visa. I sold the gold I had faithfully saved for U.S. dollars and bought a plane ticket for New York. With all that I had squirreled away, I still had about $2,000 to travel with.

Then I went to my parents to tell them of my leaving. I presented the idea as something of a white lie. I told them the trip was entirely on behalf of the factory. I didn't mention the soldier and his wife and baby and the nanny position. They would not have given their consent to let me travel to a strange man's house a half a world away. But of course I would have gone anyway, which would have created a rift that I feared might have been irreparable. It was far better to withhold the truth.

My parents weren't surprised by my announcement. My mother had been worried about me in Turkey, of course. There was her fear of me not finding a husband, but, with my ideas about making a better life for myself than the life of the typical Turkish woman, I was also in danger of falling in with the feminist movement that was emerging in the city at that time. Feminists were regarded with much disfavor by the vast majority of Turks. But I didn't consider myself a feminist. I had no desire to spend my life trying to change Turkish culture. I was pragmatic. My idea was to change my own life, not anybody else's.

And so my mother must have been terribly conflicted. I did not seem to belong in Turkey and yet what mother wants her daughter to leave? She said really none of what must have been on her mind when I told her and my father of my leaving. As a woman, it was not her place to say anything. That job fell to my father. All my mother could do was cry.

For my father's part, he no doubt thought back to his own missed opportunity to go to

Germany. In me, he saw the opportunity he was unable to realize. I could be a sort of vicarious second chance. But of course he was worried for his daughter as any father would be. "Keep your return ticket," he said. "If you have any problems, you know you will always have a home here, and home is always better than the streets, no matter what country you're in."

The next day I met up with the soldiers and I told Joel I was ready to leave anytime he and his wife were ready. "I have my visa!" I announced. And it was then that I discovered that Joel's offer had been made not out of sincerity, but misplaced kindness.

"Oh, no," Joel said through Hakan. "My wife would divorce me if I took you back home."

"You said I could be your nanny!"

"Well, you could be...but...I mean...we don't really need a nanny...my wife..." he stumbled, finally asking incredulously, "How did you even *get* a visa?"

I began to cry and soon I began to yell. Faster than Hakan could translate, I screamed, *"I got my hopes up! I went to my boss! I got my visa! I told my family – even lied to them!"* I crumpled to the ground sobbing.

"What is she saying?" asked Dale, one of the other soldiers. "Why is she crying?"

"She is ready to go the United States," said Hakan. "She has her visa and everything. She was counting on it. She thought she could go."

Joel was looking at me blankly. He didn't know what to say and there really wasn't anything he could have said anyway.

"Can't she still go?" asked Dale.

"She has no job," said Hakan, "she has no place to stay. How would she get along?"

"Well, look," said Dale, "Tell her I'll call my parents. It's possible they'd be willing to take her in for a couple months. Would that be okay?"

Hakan translated but now I was leery. Was this another empty promise? I tried not to get my hopes up. But Dale was true to his word. His parents lived in a place called Fairfield, California, not far from San Francisco. When he contacted them, they said they would enjoy hosting a for-eigner, especially a friend of Dale's. There was an English-as-Second-Language (ESL) course at the local community college that I could enroll in. Maybe I could even get a part-time job.

It appeared as if I would be going to America after all.

CHAPTER FOUR

From Sea to Shining Sea

THE PLAN WOULD BE FOR Dale to fly ahead. He had leave coming up. He would fly to San Francisco on a military transport plane and help his parents prepare for my stay in their home in Fairfield. I would keep my plane ticket to New York, then, upon arrival, I'd buy a ticket to fly from New York to San Francisco, which, I was assured, would be easy and relatively cheap.

When the day came, I flew out of Istanbul early on a June morning on a Pan Am jumbo jet, my first time on an airplane. All of my worldly belongings were in a small suitcase in the belly of the plane. I was nervous but excited. Sitting next to me on the plane out of Atatürk International Airport was an American professor who'd been teaching in Istanbul. He was on his way to visit his family back in New York. The professor knew just enough Turkish, and I knew just enough English, that we could converse, at least in an elementary fashion. He was impressed that I was making the trip. "Good for you," he said.

The flight went through Frankfurt, and from there it was an eight-hour flight to New York, arriving in the late afternoon. I tried to sleep, but I was too keyed up to doze off for more than a few minutes at a time. My mind was racing with what I imagined I would see and experience in the United States. On our approach to JFK, the plane circled above Manhattan and the pilot announced that out of the window could be seen the Statue of Liberty. I gazed out at the symbol that had beckoned so many immigrants and I could not prevent myself from crying.

"Welcome to America," the professor warmly smiled.

Then the professor, sensing my uncertainty as we exited the plane, helped me through baggage claim and customs, where my passport was stamped with a six-month grant of stay. Then he walked me over to a Pan Am ticket counter to inquire about airfare to San Francisco. But the price was too steep. Five hundred and twenty dollars. More than a quarter of all of the money I had.

"Is there a bus instead?" I said, in Turkish. "*Otobüs?*"

The professor understood and thanked the girl behind the Pan Am counter and then he ushered me outside to where the buses were lined up.

"This one," he said, pointing, "will take you to the Port Authority Bus Terminal. Once there, look for the Greyhound counter. The one with the dog? Greyhound. Tell them you want a ticket to San Francisco." He spoke slowly and repeated the instructions a few times until he was satisfied I understood. Then, for good measure, he stepped into the bus and spoke to the driver. "Make sure she gets off at the Port Authority," he said.

I got on the bus and sat behind the driver and waved goodbye to the professor, wondering what I would have done without his kindness. By then, evening had come and the sun was going down and I found myself mesmerized by the lights of the city as the bus made its way into Manhattan. Already I could tell I was somewhere considerably different than from where I'd come.

Once at the Port Authority ("This is it, miss," the bus driver had turned and said to me), I managed to find the Greyhound terminal and secure a seat on a bus to San Francisco for $130. The bus would leave in an hour, giving me enough time to find something to eat. I walked around the terminal until I found a sandwich shop. Behind the counter was a large lighted menu board with only one word I could understand: *Turkey*.

"Turkey!" I said to the girl cheerfully, elated by the idea that one could buy a Turkish sandwich in the United States. Perhaps things were not so unfamilar, after all. But "turkey," I would quickly learn, had a surprising duel meaning. Still, I was a hungry traveler and the *hindi* sandwich, as I knew it, was more than satisfying.

The bus left the station at 10:00 p.m. But for short catnaps, I'd been awake for the past forty-eight hours and once seated and underway, I quickly fell asleep, only waking when the bus reached its destination the following morning. This, I naturally assumed to be San Francisco. I walked down the steps of the bus and showed the driver the tickets I had been issued to make certain I was in the right place.

"No, no, no," he said. "You have fourteen tickets there, miss. That means you have fourteen stops. It's a long ways to San Francisco. A *long* ways. This is Cleveland." I looked at him per-plexedly. "Cleveland, Ohio," he continued. "Now, at each stop, you'll have to get off and then get back on the bus, handing in the next ticket. All the way to San Francisco. See?"

I understood, although I was incredulous. We had driven through the night and there are few destinations within Turkey that you cannot get to by driving through the night.

"You have three more days and two more nights," the driver said, handing me back the tickets.

I climbed back aboard the bus realizing that I wasn't going to be arriving in San Francisco even close to when Dale and his family would be expecting me. The plan had been for me to call them from the San Francisco airport when I arrived there, certainly no later than the day after my landing in New York. Now, I was going to be showing up three days later, and at the bus depot instead of the airport. Worse, I had no idea how to make a long-distance call to California and therefore no way to let them know of my change in schedule. I could do nothing but settle into my seat.

For three days, out of the window of that Greyhound bus, I watched the United States of America roll by. If I had been nervous but excited on the plane ride, the bus trip was even more of an adventure. We rode directly through the American heartland: Indiana through Illinois and on to St. Louis and over the Mississippi River. Through the flatlands of Kansas and into the mountains of Colorado. Past Salt Lake and through the desert landscape of Nevada. I sat by the window taking it all in. At night, with little to see but perhaps the lights of some small town or another, I would try to sleep. During the day, I would soak in the scenery and marvel at the sheer size of the country. Each state seemed to me to be the size of the whole of Turkey.

It was, in fact, the first time I grasped what was meant by the name "United *States* of America." I would see the "Welcome to" signs at each state line and it was as though we'd be entering a separate country. It was like a giant Western Europe with each state the size of a nation. But one state kept leading to the next and it appeared to be never-ending. I had studied geography in school, of course, and I had seen maps of North America and I had glimpsed the United States on the globe that sat in the back of the classroom. But until I witnessed the highway rolling ceaselessly underneath the Greyhound as it made its way from state border to state border, I had not conceived of the scale.

We rode through crowded urban areas and we rode through miles of nothing but fields or forests. In Kansas I saw acres of cornfields and farms that seemed to me to be bigger than entire Turkish provinces. There were huge tractors and there were long rows of rolling irrigation equipment that was resting on wheels larger than the wheels of our bus. I thought back to the small family farms on the outskirts of Istanbul, crops being picked by hand and loaded onto the backs of mules.

Riding through the Rocky Mountains was like riding through heaven and I thought to myself that I must have been dreaming. Salt Lake City was beautiful and clean and modern. Past Lake Tahoe the June air was warm but I could see snow on the ground in spots. Everything was magical and even the desert seemed full of life, with green scrub brush where I had expected nothing but sand, imagining that all deserts were like the pictures I had seen of the Sahara. All along the way, the highway was landscaped. Flowers grew in the median. They didn't grow flowers along highways back in Turkey. I sat wide-eyed, a child in a candy store that traversed three time zones.

With my suitcase under the bus, I traveled in the same clothes I had put on in Istanbul. For three day I went without showering, without brushing my teeth. And I would grab meals when I could, at food shops in the bus stations along the way, ordering nothing but turkey sandwiches all the way to San Francisco.

CHAPTER FIVE

Man and Wife

PEOPLE WOULD COME AND GO in the seat next to mine as the bus made its various stops along the way. An elderly lady, a college student, a young man with long hair and a guitar, a monk of some sort in an orange robe. Towards Reno, a black man, maybe in his thirties, sat next to me and tried to start a conversation, but realized quickly that my grasp of English was limited. Still, I decided to show him the paper on which I had written the phone number of Dale's parents.

"Do you need to call this number?" he asked.

I nodded.

"Okay, I'll help you."

At the stop in Reno, we got off the bus and found a pay phone. He dialed the number, placing a collect call, and Dale's mother answered. Then the man explained to her where I was and, glancing at my ticket, let her know when I'd be arriving at the San Francisco Greyhound station. I would learn later how worried Dale's family had been. His parents hadn't slept. Of course they had no way to contact me. All they knew was that I'd arrived in New York and they could only assume I'd become hopelessly lost somewhere.

"Thank you," I told the man and we boarded the bus again.

From Reno, it was five hours to San Francisco, including stops in Sacramento and Oakland. Finally we arrived at the depot where Dale and his younger brother Tom were waiting for us. Dale was smiling, relieved.

It was about an hour's drive to Fairfield and Dale's house in a nice, middle-class neighborhood with clean homes and neat lawns. Nothing, in other words, like my neighborhood outside of Istanbul. Besides Tom, Dale also had an older brother – Joe who lived close by with his wife Vicky and their five-year-old daughter Melodie. And I would learn there was a sister. Sheryl, married with two kids, lived in Southern California.

Dale's parents – Dorville and Joanne – smiled warmly at me upon our arrival and we conversed with gestures and small words. Dorville was tall and thin; Joanne was petite with short curly blonde hair. I could see that Dale, who was around five-feet-nine, physically took more after his mother than his father. I would learn that his personality was more like his mother's, too. Dorville was outgoing and talkative while Joanne, like her son, was quiet and reserved.

It was late in the evening by the time I'd arrived and I was desperate for some sleep in a real bed. Joanne showed me my room. It had been Dale's when he'd grown up there. Small, with a single bed and a chest of drawers and a closet. Luxurious by Turkish standards. Dale, meanwhile, home for a few more days of leave, would sleep on the living room couch. Tom still lived at home and had the third of the three bedrooms. There were two bathrooms in the house, a kitchen, dining room, and a fenced-in backyard. It may as well have been a palace.

The next morning my education on American culture began with an introduction to packaged breakfast cereal: Cheerios, to be exact. I was also given options that went by the names of Frosted Flakes and Froot Loops, neither of which were like anything I had seen in Turkey, at least not in our small village. Over the course of the next several weeks, I would learn much about living in the United States. Everything seemed magical to me. I marveled at the switch on the living room wall that could make the house cool, even in the summer heat of Fairfield. Cold air would blow out of vents in the ceiling. And I was assured the same wall device would cause hot air to come out of those same vents in the winter. Our house in Turkey had been heated by a central stove and even the newer apartments in Istanbul only made use of old-style radiated heat.

Joanne took me shopping and I marveled once again, first at the front doors of the local Safeway which slid open automatically as we approached them, and then more so by the size of the store and the rows and rows of food. In Turkey, each day you would buy the ingredients for your family's dinner, typically at some small family-run shop that you would walk to. I watched Dale's mother load up a grocery cart full of food that would go onto pantry shelves and into their large refrigerator, enough of it to last a week or more.

There were ESL classes that would begin in the fall, not far from Dale's house, at a community college. These were free adult-education classes. Until then, I satisfied myself trying to learn the language as best I could with the help of Dale's parents. I committed to trying to learn fifty new words a day, an unrealistic goal. Still, I made fair progress learning the names of household items, days of the week, colors, foods, and the like. In the afternoons, Joanne and I would watch soap operas where they seemed to speak more slowly than on other television programs and I was able to pick up on the dialogue often by the context and the facial expressions. But I knew I had a long way to go.

With Dale back at Çakmaklı army base, Tom took me around Fairfield, introducing me to his friends. It was hard at first as my meager vocabulary left me much too shy and self-conscious to say anything but the most basic of phrases, but everyone was friendly and welcoming. In time, Tom and I would become like brother and sister and it was good to have someone closer to my age to interact with on a daily basis.

Dale's father was retired from the Air force, but worked as a civilian at McClellan Air Force Base in Sacramento. Although he'd had a physical deformity that caused him to limp, he'd still managed to make it into the Air Force. He had tested exceptionally well and was highly skilled mechanically. After his retirement, the Air Force found a way to keep him around.

Dorville and Joanne were extraordinarily nice to me, allowing me to tag along with them when they'd run errands, taking me with them to church every Sunday and taking me to church picnics. With three sons, and a daughter who lived several hours away, I imagined they appreciated having a girl around the house that they could treat like another daughter. They were generous, never asking for a dime from me. For my part, I helped Joanne as much as possible, lending a hand with dinner, doing laundry, cleaning up the house.

Often we'd go out to dinner and at first the only thing I felt comfortable ordering was chicken because I knew the word and it seemed, in one form or another, to be on the menu of any restaurant we'd go to. Fried chicken confused me at first because I hadn't seen breaded foods before. I'd peel off the outer coating and I'm sure the rest of the family must have thought I didn't care for it, but the opposite was the case once I tried it.

Once we all went to Six Flags Amusement Park in Vallejo and another time we drove down to Los Angeles where Joanne had a sister. We met their daughter Sheryl there, too. I stared open-mouthed at the people and the sights of Hollywood and the homes of Beverly Hills.

It was much too expensive to place a phone call home, but I wrote, probably not as often as I should have. I didn't have the words to describe all that I was discovering about America, though I tried. "The people are very kind," I told my parents, "and you should see the homes here!"

Joe and Vicky and five-year-old Melodie would come over often. Melodie and I became good friends. Her understanding of English was about as elementary as mine, after all, and we were able to converse surprisingly well with our limited vocabularies of small words. I noticed the same thing at the church picnics where the smaller kids would gravitate towards me and we'd play tag – me, a nineteen-year-old chasing and being chased by toddlers, all of us having a great time and chatting with each other as best we could with our respective versions of broken English.

In the fall, the ESL classes began and I soaked up everything I could. Dorville showed me where the city bus would pick me up and every day I would ride it to the school. The classes started in the mornings and went into the early afternoons. In addition to teaching the language, they taught us about the culture. We learned some of the history and we learned about American holidays. We learned about American units of measurement, too – ounces and pounds instead of grams.

Most of the people at the school were Asian or Mexican. There was nobody from Turkey. It was a blessing. During breaks, everyone would split into their own groups, talking their native language to one another. But for me to be able to converse with anybody, I was forced to use English, even during the breaks. From the time I landed in New York, except for the letters I would write home, there was never a reason for me to use my native language. And so after just a couple of months of the ESL classes, I was speaking conversational English if not fluently, at least with some confidence.

But by mid October, I knew I had a problem. I wanted to stay in America. I could not conceive of going back to Turkey. I had seen too much. I could imagine nothing but opportunity in the United States and there was virtually nothing about the country that I didn't like. Mr. Aykaç had been right: "If you go, you will not come back," he had said. And yet my visa was set to expire in December. I thought about leaving and coming back into the country again. I knew that people did this a lot. If I went to Mexico or Canada, I could re-enter under another six-month visa. But I realized this was no long-term solution. I couldn't keep asking Dorville and Joanne to take me to Mexico every six months just so I could come back into the States. And how long could I expect to stay with them, anyway?

Dale called one day from Çakmaklı and we talked and I explained my dilemma, about how I was going to have to leave. "Dale," I told him, "I don't want to go back. I want to stay in this country."

"Well, maybe we can work something out," he said. Then, after a long pause, he said, "Look, Emi, I'm going to see if I can get leave. I'll come home. I think I have a solution, if you want it."

"What solution?" I asked.

"Well, you could...you could marry me."

As Dale's wife, I could become a naturalized citizen. For a poor girl from Turkey the prospect was thrilling. I knew nothing about love. I'd had no boyfriends. In Turkey, a young woman wouldn't have a boyfriend. A family would never allow a daughter to be alone with a man. My future was either as a perpetually single woman – an eventual spinster – or as the wife of a man who would not be of my choosing. With Dale, I would be marrying a genuinely good man, a man I liked, from a wonderful family. Although I didn't find him especially attractive, he was sweet and kind and honest. I knew I would be safe and secure. I thought of my parents. They hadn't been in love, and yet they had made a marriage work very well. Best of all, I would become a U.S. citizen. I said yes immediately.

Dorville and Joanne were just as happy with the prospect. Dale was twenty-seven and had never really had a girlfriend. His whole life, he'd been shy around girls. Now, he was going to have a wife. Dorville and Joanne genuinely liked me and believed the marriage would be perfect for us both.

I later learned that Dale's older brother would question Dale about the marriage. "Are you sure she's not just using you?" Joe had asked him. Obviously that was not an uncommon thing. I had heard about people charging upwards of two-thousand dollars to allow themselves to be married so that their new spouse could become a citizen. And then, of course, the couple would get divorced. In my more desperate moments, thinking about the possibility of having to go back to Turkey, never to return to the U.S., the possibility had crossed my mind. But of course I didn't have the money, anyway. And besides, Dale was a more than suitable candidate for me. A better prospect than I could ever have imagined finding in Turkey. Dale would allow me freedom. My interest in Dale was sincere and Dale managed to assure Joe of it.

As for my parents, Dale went to see them with a translator, getting their blessing. He understood enough about Turkish culture to know the necessity of doing so. My mother called me shortly afterwards. It was an expensive call that she felt was worth the cost.

"Are you sure, Emi?" she said. "You have always said you never wanted to be tied down. It's why you left here." It was hard for me to explain to my mother that in the United States, marriage was another form of freedom. It was an opportunity, not a constraint. I could be a wife and still do what I wanted to do.

"It's not like Turkey," I said, before changing tack: "Besides, you met him. Isn't he nice? And his family has been great to me. Very generous. I'll be well taken care of."

Dale flew back to the States in late October on an army transport for a one-week leave. The wedding was a small family affair at the church, followed by a modest reception. There would be no honeymoon; Dale had to return to Çakmaklı. But his parents arranged for a room at the Hilton for our wedding night. We were man and wife. And I was a step closer to becoming a United States citizen.

CHAPTER SIX

Citizen

DALE RETURNED FOR CHRISTMAS having been re-assigned to the States. He had big news: we would be moving to Seneca Army Depot in New York. In my mind, New York meant New York City and I found myself excited by the possibilities. I remembered Manhattan from the bus trip. I'd seen New York City in movies, television shows, pictures in magazines. "Well, it's *upstate* New York," I was told, but I had no idea how big the state of New York was. New York was New York.

In January of 1985, we packed all of our stuff into a rented U-Haul and drove east, mostly on the same highways on which I had traveled west in the Greyhound just seven months prior. It was hard saying goodbye to Dale's parents and everyone else I'd met in California, everyone who had been so nice to me. Dorville and Joanne had become like family, even before the wedding that had made it official. But I was young and the move was another adventure for me. A great American adventure.

But upstate New York is cold in January. That's the first thing that made an impression on me. I hated the cold, remembering as a child having to walk to school on frigid mornings without proper clothes or shoes. I had never wanted to be cold again. The trees were all bare and most of the days seemed gray and dismal. There was snow and it seemed to me that if it wasn't snowing, it was raining. There never seemed to be any other kind of weather. New York was nothing like California.

Located in the Finger Lakes region of New York, Seneca was small and so were all the surrounding towns. The closest thing to a city was Rochester, an hour and half away. For the record, New York City was a six-hour drive. Two-hundred and fifty miles that might as well have been a million.

For a few days and nights we stayed with a nice couple who worked with the base, acting as a kind of host family for newly-arriving base personnel. Then we were moved to a hotel for a couple of nights while a rental house Dale found was being readied for us. The rental house was in nearby Lodi and Lodi was even smaller than Seneca. The house sat right on one of the lakes but the beauty of the setting was lost on me in the cold winter. And in the feeling of isolation.

It didn't help that I'd not been feeling well. Since we'd arrived in Seneca, I'd been feeling nauseous and tired. A couple weeks went by and I was not getting better. I went to see a doctor and received news I was in no way prepared for: I was pregnant. Dale was excited. He'd turned twenty-eight in December. He was ready to start his family. He had his military career, his small-town home, his wife, and now a baby on the way.

I was nineteen, my twentieth birthday still a month away. I'd come over to the United States from Turkey to escape a life of limited options. Just a few weeks earlier, in California, there was nothing but opportunity ahead of me. My head had reeled from the possibilities and the excitement of a blank slate that I could fill however I'd wanted. Now, abruptly, the excitement stopped. I could feel my dreams dying. I could sense the opportunities drifting away into the cold gray of upstate New York. I told Dale I didn't want to have the baby.

"But...you have to," he said. "You're not...are you thinking of an abortion? Emi, I don't believe in that. None of us do. We're a religious family, Emi. Abortion isn't allowed."

Dale no doubt believed he was giving me a

good life. He knew where I had come from, he knew of the poverty and the lack of opportunity in Turkey. But what I'd been unable to communicate to him, mostly because of my lack of English, but also because of my inability, at nineteen, to define it even for myself, was the concept I had in my mind of the life of a self-sufficient woman. I had ideas that included advanced schooling and a career. In what, I wasn't sure. Probably something in the design field, given my experience in Istanbul in the textile industry. Dale naturally assumed I'd be happy as an American housewife. And so there I was, married, living in a foreign country, completely dependent on my husband, and given no choice but to continue the pregnancy.

Settling into the area, I decided I'd continue learning English. The couple who rented us our house in Lodi happened to be teachers at the local high school and I asked them if they thought anybody would mind if I sat in on some classes. They said it would be fine and I began attending the school, sitting in on English classes as well as home economics classes where I learned cooking. The classes helped me feel a little better, a little more alive and less stagnant. The other students thought it was "cool" that a person from a foreign country, older than high school age, and pregnant, was taking the time to attend classes of her own accord. I even made a few friends.

School let out early in the afternoon, but Dale, who would drive me to school in the morning, worked at the base until late in the day. It was too far for me to walk home from the school so I would have to wait for Dale with nothing to do. Next to the school was a pharmacy owned by a man from India and one day I decided to try putting my waiting time to good use. I walked into the pharmacy and asked the owner if he needed any part-time help. He thought for a moment and told me that, yes, as a matter of fact, he could use some help stocking the shelves every afternoon.

The job only paid minimum wage, but the man seemed happy to help out a fellow foreigner. I had noticed a distinct difference in the way foreign-born people seemed to be treated in upstate New York as compared to California. People in California seemed much more open and welcoming. The people in the small towns around the Finger Lakes seemed more withdrawn, more closed to outsiders. It wasn't anything overt. Just a sense that I got from them. And of course it didn't help that I was still learning the language.

Working, even for minimum wage, gave me a way to put aside some money of my own. In the back of my mind was the idea of returning to Turkey. Not to stay, but to at least visit. By then, I had begun to miss my parents and the country in which I'd grown up. I missed home. But the pharmacy job ended with the end of the school year in May. I couldn't get any more hours, and there was no transportation to the store available for me in the afternoon from our house on the lake. That summer I learned to drive, but we could only afford one car, the car Dale drove every day to the base. And so all summer I was stuck at the house.

In September I gave birth to our son. Matthew was a beautiful boy and like any mother, I felt a close bond. But my days soon became nothing but taking care of him and keeping the house while Dale was off at the base. I had no life. No friends. No means of transportation. My feelings of isolation increased. I felt lonely and cut off from the world. I was miserable.

Dale knew I was unhappy.

"Listen," he said, "I have an idea. Let's move to Geneva. It's just as close to the base but it's a bigger town. We could get an apartment downtown so you'd be in walking distance to things. You could get out more. Maybe get a part-time job. Go to school. Whatever you want, Emi."

We moved to the town of Geneva, about a

half an hour away, and it was a definite improvement from the secluded house on the lake outside of Lodi. I was determined to find work and went to a temp agency where they found me a night-shift job on an assembly line at a manufacturing facility. Zotos International made beauty products and my job was in quality control, making sure the ink on the labels that were affixed to the shampoo bottles wasn't smeared before the bottles were boxed for shipment. The night work meant that I could watch Matthew during the day while Dale watched him at night.

But it also meant, since Matthew slept mostly at night, that I got very little sleep during the day. I was becoming exhausted and I soon quit the assembly line work at Zotos and took a position at a nearby hotel as a maid. It was a few hours a day and for that time, we were able to find daycare for Matthew. But after a month or so, I quit that job too. I hadn't traveled halfway around the globe – all the way from Istanbul, Turkey – to clean toilets. That wasn't part of the dream. But realistically, what could I do? What was I qualified for?

At one point I tried to enroll in a cosmetology school but part of the application process included a basic English test. I failed it. Finally I found a job at a Friendly's Restaurant within walking distance of our apartment. With tips, the waitresses made the good money. But my English wasn't good enough for me to be able to converse with the customers so I was put to work in the kitchen during the breakfast shift, making omelets and pancakes and hash browns. No matter how long I would shower after coming home from my shift, I always seemed to smell like food.

A year went by. My life was a dead-end. By the summer of 1986, Dale knew I was no happier than I'd been in Lodi. He was frustrated and I was still miserable and we were now both unhappy. He knew, too, that I was missing home and my parents. He requested a transfer – back to Turkey.

"Maybe you'll be happier back there," he said. "It'll give you a little time to figure out what you want. You'll be back home where you can relax a little, see your family. It'll do us both good. It'll be a good break. We'll spend a year or so there and then figure out what to do."

The idea was very appealing to me. I had no interest in remaining more than the year Dale was proposing. I was committed to a future in the United States but I needed some time to think, time to figure out what I really wanted to do, time away from my cheerless, monotonous life in upstate New York.

Before we left for Turkey, there was one
thing I wanted to take with me, one thing I would
not leave the United States without: my citizenship. I wanted more than just a passport. I wanted
to make certain I'd be admitted back when we
would eventually make our return. I sensed the
possibilities America offered, even if I was not at
that time realizing those possibilities. I knew
there would eventually be a better life for me and
that better life was in the United States, not
Turkey and not in any other country. Citizenship
meant freedom. I could travel anywhere in the
world and still be admitted back to the U.S. at
any time. There would no longer be any limita-
tions or stipulations. I would no longer have to
enter the country as a guest. The United States
would be my home.

I went to Rochester and took my Natural-
ization test – a three-part exam: English, U.S. history, and civics. And then, on a cold, rainy day, I
stood before a judge in a Rochester courtroom
with about twenty other new citizens and took
the oath of allegiance to "...support and defend
the Constitution and laws of the United States of
America..."

I was now a citizen.

CHAPTER SEVEN

Pre-med and Potatoes

AFTER I GOT MY CITIZENSHIP, Dale and I packed up a U-Haul and drove back to California to leave all of our stuff with Dale's parents. We spent a few days with them and then we moved back to the country of my birth.

We got an apartment in the Istanbul neighborhood of Florya, next to the Sea of Marmara. We could walk to the beach. Dale stayed at the base during the week and would come home to the apartment on weekends. My brothers and sister would visit and I would spend time with my parents as well. Everybody enjoyed seeing Matthew. It was good being home.

At the army base, where I'd be invited for picnics and get-togethers, I made a few friends. One soldier, Scott, was attracted to me but knew I was married. "Do you have any friends or sisters?" he asked. I told him of my sister Naime and arranged to have the two meet, acting as translator. The two hit it off and began to see a lot of each other. But, as I explained to Scott, this was Turkey, not the United States. "You know you cannot sleep with my sister," I said. "Not unless you marry her." Before long, Scott would do just that and, like me, my sister was soon married to an American.

Although it was good to see everyone that I had left behind, Turkey presented nothing new to me. It was as I had left it. There was no future for me there, no opportunity. I wanted to go back to the United States, but I knew it had to be on different terms. If I returned to America, there could be no coming back to Turkey again. I couldn't bear the thought of coming home a failure, unable to find, or make, the life I had wanted in the States. If I was committed to making a life in America, it had to be on my terms.

One evening, I spoke to Dale.

"Dale," I said, "I want to go back but I don't want to go back to cleaning bathrooms in hotels or cooking in a Friendly's. These are good, solid jobs. But I want something more. I need to go to school. I need to further my education. I want a future with more potential for me. Let's find somewhere where I can have that. And no cold places!" Dale agreed and managed to secure a transfer to Redstone Army Base in Huntsville, Alabama. Huntsville was a bigger city than Geneva. And warmer.

Meanwhile, Dale and I weren't the only ones thinking of traveling to the United States. Scott was looking to get transferred back home and taking his new bride with him. Naturally I encouraged Namie. It would be good for her, I told her. Good to stretch herself beyond the culture of our upbringing. Our mother felt differently. "Naime is not you," she told me. "Your sister won't like the independence of America the way that you do. She won't make it there."

"You don't give her enough credit," I insisted. "She will love America."

Dale and I stayed in Turkey about a year, but after that, it was time to go back to the land of opportunity. We said our goodbyes to my family and left. Shortly afterwards, Naime's husband managed to get a transfer to Olympia, Washington. Now both my sister and I were living in the U.S.

In Huntsville, Dale and I got an apartment. I began going to school but all I could find was a community college in Decatur, Alabama – Calhoun Community College, about a half an hour away. I took basic courses, not entirely certain of what field I wanted to go into. Design was still on my mind, but what I was finding was that I seemed to do best in math courses, and science courses like chemistry and physics where proficiency in English wasn't necessary. There was very little reading. Formulas are formulas. Two plus two equals four in every language in the world. Before long it occurred to me that I could take those courses and start working my way towards a profession in the medical field. Doctors were always in demand, after all. A future as a doctor seemed full of promise.

There was something else that factored into the decision. By then I'd had more than enough experience in getting turned down for jobs by people who make snap decisions based on a person's accent or where they're from. A person with a medical degree commands more respect, even authority. And as a doctor, I knew I could eventually have my own practice where I'd be the one doing the hiring. Medicine was going to be my path to independence.

But the days were long and tiring. I needed the car to get to Decatur so I would drop Dale off at Redstone in the morning, drop the baby off at the base daycare, then go to class. The daycare cost money, however, and Dale's salary wouldn't pay for much more than the apartment and food. I needed to work. So after coming home in the afternoon, and picking up Dale and Matthew, I would then go to a job I had found working check-out at a Toys "R" Us. My hours were from five o'-clock until nine every evening, at which time I'd come home and study until late.

For two years this represented my life. And yet I felt I was getting nowhere. For one thing, I knew that to advance in medicine, I needed to go to a quality medical school. Huntsville didn't have one. And even before that, I would need a pre-med degree, something Calhoun didn't offer. I started thinking about something else, too. I be-gan to wonder what would happen if Dale got transferred, something very common, of course, with a military career. If we went elsewhere, would I have to start my coursework all over again? I couldn't even hold onto the hope that we'd be transferred somewhere with more op-portunity – a bustling city somewhere with a uni-versity. It seems that army bases are generally lo-cated in small towns. I was feeling trapped once again. I was becoming depressed and Dale felt it, too. The marriage suffered.

All the while, my sister was feeling some-thing similar, but for different reasons. Naime had had a baby girl and she was more content than I was to remain a housewife and mother. But she missed Turkey and our parents terribly. She hadn't made the effort I had made to learn the language and she made few friends and had virtually no life outside of her husband and daughter. Our mother had been right. Naime was not me. She had not been as cut out for a move to a foreign land, even one with the opportunities that the United States presented; the opportunities were essentially lost on her. Eventually, Scott left the military and he and Naime and the baby moved from Washington State to Appleton, Wisconsin to be closer to his family. It gave her a wider circle of acquaintances, but it was hard for Naime to get close to anybody. The language and culture were both stumbling blocks for her and she remained unhappy.

I was unhappy, too, and it was time to talk to Dale about it, about my future, about our marriage.

"I have to move forward," I told him. "I have to get out of here, Dale. I've done some research. The University of Alabama at Birmingham has an undergraduate pre-med program and a medical school. I can be a doctor, Dale. But I can't do it here."

"But...UAB must be a hundred miles from here. What are you planning on doing with Matthew?"

"I can't take him with me. I can't be a full-time mother and a fulltime medical student. It wouldn't be fair to Matthew. He needs more than that. I've talked with my parents and they've agreed they can take him for us while I'm in school."

"But that's not fair to Matthew, either," Dale said. "Emi, he needs his parents. Or at the least, one of us. Look, I won't stop you from going, Emi. If that's what you're set on doing, I'm not going to stand in your way. But leave Matthew with me. I'll take him."

I agreed. It was what I had hoped Dale would say. I knew it was the best decision for Matthew as well as for Dale. My parents were a decent backup plan, but I wanted Matthew to be with his father. Still, there was a larger issue and Dale and I both knew it. My going away was not going to be a temporary thing. By then, we were going in completely different directions. Dale was now in his thirties and content to settle down. I was just twenty-four, still at the beginning of my adulthood, with dreams of an exciting future. Besides Matthew, Dale and I had almost nothing in common and we both knew the marriage had to end. I would always be grateful to Dale and to his family for providing me a path to United States citizenship, but the time had come for me to move on. Dale understood. We got a divorce and in early August of 1989, I moved to Birmingham and enrolled in the University of Alabama.

I bought a used car that I financed for $200 a month. Dale – always kind, always willing to do the right thing – was good enough to help with a small studio apartment, giving me enough money to pay the security deposit and first month's rent. I couldn't bring myself to ask for anything more, even though I knew the small amount of cash I had saved would not nearly be enough.

I applied for, and received, a Pell Grant. That would help pay tuition, but it wouldn't kick in until the start of school, still more than a month away. And even then, for expenses beyond tuition, I knew I'd need a part-time job. I applied everywhere for a retail position including J.C. Penney, Sears, and Macy's. I filled out application after application. I heard nothing back.

By the time classes began, I was almost completely out of money. I held onto as much of my savings as I could, knowing I had to make rent and pay the car payment. Often I ate only once a day. I'd buy a bag of potatoes that would last me for a week or more. One day I'd have a baked potato, the next I'd have fried potatoes, the day after that I'd have boiled potatoes. I knew nobody to ask for help. I thought about calling my parents for a loan, but I knew they didn't have enough money as it was. I was becoming desperate, and worried.

Eventually, I applied for food stamps, but was told I didn't qualify: I had no dependents. Plus, I had assets.

"You can sell your car," the woman at the social services office suggested.

"Then how will I get to school?" I asked.

"I'm sorry," she said. "We can't help you."

At one point, close to penniless, I contemplated digging for food through dumpsters behind restaurants. Briefly crossing my mind were other things a young woman could do to make money.

By then, I'd made a friend at school named Dawn. I confided in her one day how hard it was for me to make ends meet, how I couldn't get a job, how I was living in relative poverty.

"Why don't you sign up for ROTC?" she said. "They pay a hundred dollars a month." The Pell Grant took care of tuition but I still had rent coming due as well as the car payment. It wouldn't cover everything, but a hundred bucks was a hundred bucks. With that, I was sure I could find a way to make it. And it wasn't as if I was unfamiliar with the military. I joined ROTC. I liked it. There was one ROTC class per semester plus we met every morning for P.T. – physical training. I met people and made friends and enjoyed the camaraderie.

At ROTC, it was suggested that I should join the National Guard. That required one weekend a month and it paid $250. Now I was making $350 a month. In the meantime, I left my apartment and moved on campus to the dorms which were cheaper. I was finally making ends meet, though there was very little money left over at the end of the month and I still had to be careful how I spent it. But at least I felt as if I could breathe.

Finally, in October, J.C. Penney called. There was an evening sales position open and I took it. My schedule became demanding and often stressful. There was ROTC, there was the National Guard, there were difficult pre-med courses, and there was work at J.C. Penney. But I felt as if my world was finally opening up. And at least now, for the first time in weeks, I could eat something other than potatoes.

CHAPTER EIGHT

Captain

WITH MY CREDITS FROM Calhoun Community, I needed just one year of undergraduate work at the University of Alabama at Birmingham to get accepted into the medical school – assuming my grades would be good enough. I worked hard, studying every free minute in between classes and ROTC and work at J.C. Penney. While other students were out on Friday and Saturday nights, I stayed in and studied my premed coursework. I took extra courses, as well, with some of the courses overlapping with med school, counting towards my first year. It paid off. In 1990, I finished with a 4.0 grade point average and a bachelor's degree in natural science.

Because of my ROTC commitment, I owed the army three years of service, which would be deferred until my graduation from medical school. I had taken premed classes with the idea of being an ENT. But, as it happened, the National

Guard unit I had been with was a medical detachment, and, specifically, a dental unit. I talked with some of the dentists and became interested in the profession. It seemed to me especially good for a young woman perhaps thinking one day of starting a family. Unlike ENT work, or even general medicine, you could have a lot more latitude in your schedule. You could have your appointments in the morning for example and keep your afternoons free. Or work three days a week. It seemed just right for me, and I made up my mind to go into dentistry.

But dental school was hard, harder even than my natural science coursework. And it was competitive. The students who had been accepted into UAB's dental school had, like me, all done well with their undergraduate studies. With the advanced curriculum, it seemed like I was learning yet another language. Classes were all day long, followed by time in the lab learning how to make inlays and crowns and partials. I wouldn't get home before 9:00 or 10:00 every night and was often up past 1:00 studying for the following day's quizzes or exam.

My social life was mostly non-existent, although I did manage to make a couple of good friends. I met Lory right away, in orientation, and we became study partners. Her husband was a physician from Turkey and the two had a little girl. They would invite me over and it was fun to spend time with them. Lory, because of her husband, understood my difficulties with the language and became more like a tutor than a study partner. This actually worked out well for the both of us; I learned the material while Lory received a grasp of it in the way that only teaching something can provide. I pushed her, too. With a family, she couldn't focus the way that I could and our studying together helped her do that. We drove each other.

In my second year I met Sue who had graduated from dental school in England and was doing her pedodontics residency in Birmingham. Sue was originally from Iraq and her mother was Turkish. Being from another country, she had to take some of the classes I was taking to become licensed and we became study partners, too. Between Lory and Sue, I would ultimately do well in dental school, graduating in a class from which close to twenty-percent of the enrollees would drop out. To this day I remain close friends with both Lory and Sue.

And then there was John. John had moved to Birmingham and was working in the financial services industry. We met and connected right away. Things became serious. John would take me out to nice places and he opened me up to new experiences. We ate sushi, something I'd never done. His work would entail travel and often he'd take me with him and I'd get to see places I'd never seen before.

I never went away for more than a couple of days at a time, however. I knew I needed to focus on my schoolwork. But although the instructors were demanding, I appreciated the discipline, an attitude of mine that I noticed wasn't necessarily shared by everyone. Sheryl was a friend and a classmate in a lab class. She was a black girl from Houston and she attributed every piece of constructive criticism to racism. In her mind, the instructors had it in for her. We talked a lot about it. I wanted to be sympathetic, but I didn't see racism.

"They just want us to be better," I would say. "I get criticized, too. But how else do we know when we're doing something wrong? How else will we learn? It's good for us."

"You wouldn't understand, Emi," she would say. "You didn't grow up here. You don't know how it works here. You don't know about the prejudice, especially here in the South."

"I know about prejudice. I'm a foreigner. The instructors know I'm not from here. They know I'm from the Middle East. But when they tell me I've messed something up, I don't take it to mean they're being critical of me because I'm a foreigner. Why do you think they're being critical of you because you're black?"

"You just don't understand," she would say, and there would be no talking her out of her belief that she was being discriminated against. It was a chip on her shoulder that she could never put down. Eventually, her perceptions would cause her enough stress where she would have to take a break from dental school for a few years.

Maybe it was naiveté on my part but I never saw what she saw. I had seen prejudice in my homeland. Prejudice against Sunnis or prejudice against Shias. Prejudice against women. Prejudice against outsiders, against Americans, against Christians. I found the people of the South, at least the people of Birmingham, to be nothing but nice to me, nicer even than the people of upstate New York who always seemed colder towards me. Of course by the time I was in dental school I was speaking English fairly well, even thinking and dreaming in English. Maybe that explained the aloofness of the New Yorkers who had to contend with my heavier accent. But in any event, even if I had felt prejudice from my instructors, it would not have stopped me. I had no interest in making any excuses for my work.

As long as I was learning from my instructors, I had no bones to pick.

By my final year of dental school in 1994, John had been transferred. He was originally from Minnesota and he hadn't been happy in Birmingham. He managed to get himself a position in Denver. To be close to him, my hope was to start my three-year army hitch at Fort Collins, just north of Denver, but I knew it was a popular destination spot for military people and the odds that I'd be allowed to go there were low. Fort Collins was typically reserved for those with more seniority. And so I hit upon the idea of volunteering for a tougher spot, somewhere like South Korea. I figured that after a year there, I'd have earned the right to ask for a transfer to Fort Collins.

"Well, we don't like to send newcomers overseas," I was told. "But there's a dental unit in Hawaii. How would you feel about that?"

Hawaii? I accepted in about two seconds.

But before Hawaii came basic training at Fort Sam Houston in San Antonio. With ROTC, I had come out of dental school a captain in the United States Army. And so the training was the OBLC – the Officer Basic Leadership Course. Ten weeks of physical fitness and learning the ways of the military. It was thorough and demanding.

They sent us out in the field with tents and we learned survival and navigational skills. How to dig trenches. How to properly pack a rucksack. We learned how to rappel from a helicopter. We learned how to operate M16 rifles and 9mm pistols. I loved every minute of it.

When I got to Hawaii, I earned my Expert Field Medical Badge which included complete training and testing on how to function in combat zones. It was grueling. There was a comprehensive written test and a physical fitness test. There was testing on triaging and evacuating casualties. There were day and night navigation courses you were required to traverse. There were obstacle courses and testing on survival skills and weapons. You had to show competency with field radios and communication techniques. And finally, there was a forced road march with "standard fighting load." This meant trudging for twelve miles in your heavy army clothes and boots and carrying your M16 and over forty pounds in your backpack. I finished first, receiving an award. I even beat all the male soldiers. I was able to assemble my weapon faster than the guys, too. I thought back to my discussion in high school with my uncles about *Private Benjamin*. Women shouldn't be in the army, they had said. But I had found my spot. The Army was where I belonged.

I committed to remaining in the Army beyond my three-year obligation. I liked everything about it – the organization, the discipline, the way that I was pushed to excel. And the decision was aided by the fact that I hadn't received any kind of commitment from John. He had moved to Denver and we had kept in touch, but he never spoke of marriage or our future together. "Let's see how things go," he had said. But I wasn't willing to risk giving up the Army to be with him only to learn that he had no long-term intention of marrying me. We broke up. It was heartbreaking for both of us, but apparently not enough for him to want to try to make things work. He had his life and I had mine.

In Hawaii, I rented a furnished apartment from a woman who was a retired attorney from New York. The rent was a bit steep, but I talked her into a discount for a five-year commitment from me. Arlene and I became friends. I admired her. In New York she'd been a single mother with two daughters. She was fifty when she passed her bar exam. For Arlene, it was never too late to redefine your life.

I started in Hawaii in the dental corps, commanded by Colonel Richard Shipley. Shipley had started in a helicopter unit before going to dental school and then ultimately becoming commander in Hawaii. He would eventually see how hard I worked and what I was capable of, and his encouragement would prove invaluable to me.

But my first job was working under an officer who was a prosthodontist, doing crown and bridge work. At the time, I still had the mentality of a student and was hoping I could learn from the officer, that maybe he could mentor me. Apparently, he didn't see it that way. One day, very early in my service under this officer, I had trouble with an impression of a particular soldier's mouth. But I imagined what I had done was at least sufficient for casting the crown the soldier needed. Evidently, it was not.

"Doctor, this is not a dental school!" the officer yelled at me. "We demand better work than *this!*" Then he continued to dress me down in front of everybody, the patient included. It was embarrassing. And it was far from constructive criticism, which I would have readily accepted. It was a humiliation.

An endodontist overheard the chewing-out and he approached me later. Colonel John Mc-Cann. We'd met before. He had at one time been stationed in Turkey and we had talked at length about Istanbul.

"Don't worry about him," McCann said. "How would you like to do root canals instead of crowns and bridges? I'll give you some cases. We'll start with some easy ones until you get a feel for it. Forget prosthodontics. I think you'll find me a bit more pleasant to work with."

Colonel McCann was right. I worked with him for a few weeks, learning quickly. Then one day he went on vacation and while he was gone a more complicated case than what I had worked on up until that point presented itself. McCann's assistant, who, I had observed, seemed to know as much as the colonel himself, said, "Don't worry, I'll walk you through it and we'll do it together." The procedure went smoothly, flawlessly. When the colonel came back, I told him I had found my field.

In 1996, I took a two-week leave and went to visit my parents in Turkey. I hadn't seen them since Dale and I were there in 1986-87. They were proud of me. I think my mother was pleased that I had worked my way into a position of self-sufficiency and financial security. She no longer had to worry about me. For my father's part, he was more proud that I was an officer than a doctor. The Turkish army didn't even accept women, let alone make women into officers.

After returning to Hawaii I began volunteering for humanitarian missions. A little-known fact about the United States Army is that, far from being just a fighting force, it's active in helping people around the globe that are in crisis. Earthquakes, hurricanes, famines – the U.S. Army is often the first to respond. Sometimes the missions that became available to us were not associated with any specific natural disasters; sometimes they were just focused on remote areas of extreme poverty where medical services were practically nonexistent, or where the local doctors simply didn't have the resources to be able to adequately do their jobs. We would form coalitions with those doctors and come in with equipment and expertise and, most importantly, our time. I went to places like Maldives and Mongolia. It was humbling, seeing the way the people lived. And gratifying to be able to help them.

On the Mongolia trip we flew in and out of Beijing and I got the chance to walk on the Great Wall of China. All I could do was wonder in amazement at where I was, at the opportunity that the United States Army had given me, a girl from Turkey who came over with very little money and practically no understanding of the language. Now I was seeing the world.

In Maldives we flew in and out of Singapore and I felt the same overwhelming feeling of appreciation. I was visiting places I could only ever have dreamed about in Turkey. Maldives was otherworldly. I discovered that the country is comprised of over a thousand coral islands grouped into twenty-six atolls. It's the lowest country in the world with an average elevation above sea level of under five feet. It's predominately a Muslim country and we had to take off our shoes to walk into the hospital. Some of the culture therefore seemed familiar to me. But the deep blue of the water was something I had never seen before. I took to pinching myself to make sure I wasn't dreaming.

One of our humanitarian missions involved a ship of illegals coming from China, hundreds of them, heading to the West Coast of the United States. The Navy intercepted the ship, but before sending it back, the passengers of the ship were taken to Wake Island. I went there with an entire medical unit that spent three weeks assessing the health of the passengers and tending to their medical needs.

Back in Hawaii there was an opportunity to work for the forward support battalion for the 25th Infantry Division, under Major General John Maher, who, like Colonel Shipley, would ultimately be very encouraging and helpful to me in my military career. The support battalion would supply medical services to soldiers shipping out for duty. You wanted to make sure you'd do your part right because most of the times, once they shipped out, you'd never see the soldiers again. I knew I could be the last person with any kind of dental training that they might see for a very long while.

Given the responsibilities, I worked extra hours, feeling compelled by duty to do so. It never occurred to me that that would present a problem. But shortly past 4:30 p.m., most of the other members of the team were ready to quit for the day. My continued working would sometimes mean a few of them would have to work a little later, too. They complained, and the Officer in Charge, the chief of the clinic, had me report to his office one day.

"If you keep working past hours," he said, "I'm not going to have any choice but to write you up."

"I guess I'm still kind of new to the Army," I explained. "I thought our job was to give the soldiers whatever they needed. Twenty-four seven. Isn't that our responsibility?"

"The matter is not open to debate," he said. "You're working past regular hours which you're not authorized to do. Consider yourself warned." I left his office, but I kept working the hours that I thought were necessary. A few weeks later, as promised, he wrote me up.

"You should have listened to me," he said.

"Okay," I said. "But you know, I would rather have you write me up for working too much than for not working enough. Make it say, 'She works too hard.' I'd be fine with that." A comment went into my file that I was "disrespectful."

At one point I heard there was a need for a volunteer to go to South Korea for a short tour of duty and I thought it might be good to go somewhere else for a bit. I spent a month in South Korea. In charge of the dental corps there was General John Cuddy. The general took me aside one day.

"I heard about you," he said. "I heard about your little meeting with the OIC back in Hawaii and what you said to him."

"Oh...that. Yes, well, I'm very sorry. I really hadn't meant any disrespect to him, I just —."

"Relax," he said laughing. "I like what you told him. In my estimation, he was wrong to write you up. Listen, I'm going back to the States soon, to San Antonio as Deputy Commander of the Army Medical Command at Fort Sam Houston. I'm looking for someone to be my aid. Someone like you. Would you be interested?"

I liked Hawaii, loved it, in fact, at first. But it was hard making friends there. I felt isolated. Army personnel would come and go. The native civilians were outwardly friendly and polite, but I found them difficult to get close to. There was a certain aloofness in how they related to those who weren't native Hawaiians and I always felt like an outsider. Texas seemed like a good change of scenery to me. I told the general I'd be honored to be his aid and in 1997, I left Hawaii for San Antonio.

CHAPTER NINE

Proud

I LIKED SAN ANTONIO. I had liked it back during my basic training. There was a certain spirit the people had that you couldn't help but appreciate. I had seen "Don't Mess with Texas" bumper stickers but I didn't really understand what was meant until I visited the Alamo and started learning about the history of the state. I quickly began to respect the character and pride of Texans.

Before I went to work in General Cuddy's office, I took my advanced officers' training in San Antonio. It was yet another level of accomplishment for me. Afterwards I was put on a panel that was charged with finding ways to improve the training. There were various officers who were on the panel and on the second day of meetings, I happened to be sitting next to a female colonel named Carol who was fairly new to San Antonio. On the other side of me was an officer named Scott who was married with two children and who had been in San Antonio for a couple of years. The three of us would become friends, talking during breaks and getting to know each other.

After the panel's work was completed, the three of us remained close, often meeting for lunches and dinners at places Scott would recommend. Scott was smart and funny and easygoing, confident and full of life. Tall, blond, and blue-eyed, he seemed like the prototypical American male to me. But one day he called me on the phone and there was a sense of urgency in his voice and a tone that I didn't recognize.

"I'm in trouble," he said. "I need your help."

"Scott," I said, "what's the matter?"

"I just need you here. Can you come to my place? Please?"

"Give me the directions."

I hung up and hurried to Scott's apartment. When I got there he was out on the balcony, pacing back and forth, holding a gun.

"Scott? What is it? What's wrong?"

"My wife left me," he said flatly. "She just left. She took both the kids. She's headed back to Chicago. Here. Here's the note she left for me."

What I didn't know at the time was that Scott, although he'd hidden it well, was a manic depressive, suffering from bipolar disorder. It was apparently an inherited condition. His mother suffered from it, too. So had his older and younger brothers. His brothers would find no relief from the debilitating effects of the condition. Both had committed suicide.

"Scott, come on in," I said. "Let's talk about this. It may not be the end of the world, you know? Maybe your wife just needed a little time by herself with the kids. It happens. Let's just talk about it a little. Come in. Here, can I have the gun? Okay, good. Let's just sit down."

We talked for a while and I convinced Scott to let me drive him to the psychiatric ward of the military medical center. "Let's just get some advice," I said. "Maybe they can help you think through everything." Then I called Scott's commander. Scott had been scheduled to deploy to Yugoslavia, but the deployment was obviously canceled. He would spend two weeks in the ward. I visited him every day. I felt sorry for him and I wanted to help him. There didn't seem to be anybody else.

When he was ready to be discharged he told me he couldn't go back to his place without his wife and kids, who would not be coming back. Going back to an empty apartment would be too depressing, too heartbreaking. He was afraid he'd spiral downwards again.

"Why don't you stay with me?" I suggested.

"For a little bit. A couple weeks. At least until you feel strong again." He was grateful for the offer and moved in and the arrangement seemed to suit us both. He started feeling better and I liked having him around. We had a lot in common; we both liked running and camping and bike-riding. We'd go to the gym together. We'd take hiking trips to Big Bend National Park. Besides Dale, Scott was the first man I had spent any significant time with who seemed to appreciate the things I appreciated. I could never camp and hike and bike ride with John back in Birmingham, for instance. "I'd really rather be in a hotel than a tent," he would say, turning up his nose to the idea of camping. I did manage to talk him into going whitewater rafting once, which entailed a night of camping but he hated it. And then I dated a guy in Hawaii for a short time, a fellow officer, who said that the Army provided him with more than enough opportunities to go camping. He wouldn't run with me, either, preferring to spend his time on the golf course.

Scott liked to work out with me, hike with me, bike with me. We went to Corpus Christi together one time and Carlsbad Caverns another. At Carlsbad Caverns we camped and cooked our dinner over a campfire and talked deep into the night. Over time, I started falling for Scott. I began to feel as though I'd found my soul mate. My feelings were returned: "a couple weeks" of staying at my place became six months. In time, Scott would get divorced and we would talk about marriage.

Meanwhile, I was working as personal assistant to General Cuddy, making his daily arrangements, planning his trips, helping him with his day-to-day duties. In October of 1998, I was to be sent to an American Dental Association conference in San Francisco with General Cuddy and some other officers. The Army was always well-represented at these kinds of gatherings. At the conference, there were going to be separate meetings for different groups and there was one particular happy hour event scheduled for those conference attendees from the Army. My job was to set the event up, arranging for the food and beverages, and also setting up the colors – the various flags that would stand in the flag line behind the head table.

I was sent to San Francisco ahead of the others and Scott came along with me. We scoped out the venue and then drove our rental car to an Army National Guard facility in Marin County, north of the Golden Gate Bridge, to pick up the colors. On the way back, Scott jumped into the driver's seat of the car. Five minutes after we left the Guard facility, he pulled over in front of the Marin County Courthouse.

"I have a surprise for you," he said. Scott had called ahead. In the courthouse there was a marriage license awaiting our signature and a time slot reserved for a civil wedding ceremony to be performed by the County Clerk's office. It was the most romantic thing anyone had ever done for me.

We returned from San Francisco as husband and wife and I called my parents and my sister with the news. What were the odds, we all thought, of two Turkish sisters coming to America and finding husbands both with the same first name?

Not long after our wedding, Scott's contract with the Army was up. With the episode he'd had when his wife had left him and the consequent canceled deployment, the Army wasn't keen on keeping him. Scott was going to be without a job. Meanwhile, I knew that the next year, I'd be scheduled to complete my residency requirement at Fort Gordon in Augusta, Georgia.

"Don't worry about having to leave the Army," I told Scott. "We'll go to Augusta. I'm making enough money right now for the both of us. You can take some time and figure out what you want to do. It'll be good to have some time to weigh your options."

Scott was smart and I had observed that he was also a good writer. He wrote clearly and in a very deliberate, organized way. It occurred to me that he had the mind of an attorney and I encouraged him to go to law school. "You can get back into the Army then, too," I told him. "This time as an attorney." Scott seemed to like the idea and in December of 1998, he passed the Law School Admission Test without even studying, his score well above the average.

In January of '99, I discovered I was pregnant and Scott and I were both elated. Unlike with Matthew, I was now ready to have a family. A few months later, we moved to Augusta. My residency requirement was in the form of a coop program between the Army and the Medical College of Georgia. There were classes I needed to take at the college and then training with patients at nearby clinics. By the time I started, my pregnancy was clearly apparent and my residency mentor questioned the timing of my completion of the program.

"It doesn't look like you'll be able to do it," she said. "Not with the six weeks that the Army gives you after you have the baby."

"Who says I need six weeks?" I said. "I plan on coming right back." In fact, I would deliver our son – Willem – on a Friday in October and come back to work the following Monday.

Before the baby was born, however, I began to sense a change in Scott. And a change in our marriage. He had planned to stay home with the baby while I completed my residency. But I soon came to realize that any ambition Scott might have had to follow up on a law career was essentially gone. There were no law schools in Augusta, anyway, but even if there had been, I had the sense that Scott had lost his interest in moving forward with his life. He seemed stuck and lethargic. For the most part, it seemed to me as if he was content to sit around the house and I think he would have done so even without Willem there. He was depressed and moody and cheerless. Meanwhile, I was working hard and studying long hours. I'd come home to a dreary house and a marriage that had lost any vibrancy it had once had.

At the time, I couldn't appreciate how paralyzing mental illness can be. I didn't understand that someone so outwardly intelligent and seemingly together emotionally, could nevertheless feel burdened inwardly beyond their capacity to cope. I lost patience. Looking back, it's easy to see I should not have. But I was in the midst of a demanding residency and I didn't have the time to take care of Scott, nor did I have the time to fully grasp the depths of his depression. And whether I could appreciate his problems or not, the fact was that what had originally excited me about Scott – the intelligence, the energy, the sense of humor, the easy-going confident nature – was now gone.

Meanwhile, I was paying Scott's child support. Although he was without work, he refused, out of what I could only imagine to be pride, to petition to have the payments reduced. We fought about it. And I could sense that he resented the fact that I had to make the payments, that I had to support us both. It all came to a head one day when I was eight months pregnant. Scott left. He drove off for Chicago where he had friends and where his kids were. For ten days he was gone. He returned just before Willem was born. But my love for him would never be the same.

After my residency, the Army assigned me to Germany. Scott didn't want to go and I didn't want to make him. I suggested he stay, get his law degree or maybe a PhD, and then, after my three-year commitment, I'd come back and we could start anew. In fact, Scott was accepted into a PhD program in St. Louis where his mother lived. But he declined it, deciding finally that he'd come along with me to Germany, afraid, I suppose, of losing me if we spent so much time apart. Just the same, I paid for the first year of the school in order to keep his slot open. "Maybe," I told him, "after a year in Germany, you might decide you want to go back and start school."

In Germany we lived in a house in Landstuhl, close to Ramstein Air Base in the southwest part of the country. I worked in nearby Baumholder. Scott took a position in the Army transitions office helping soldiers who were set to return to civilian life with their resumes and preparing them for job hunting. It was a good job and he made enough to where he could afford to start paying his child support again.

Scott's frame of mind seemed to improve. Working helped him. It energized him. He still had mood swings and I could never really know from one day to the next how he might be feeling but he was better overall. It also didn't hurt that we were far away from his mother in St. Louis. A manic-depressive who had lost two sons, she had exerted a lot of influence over Scott when we had lived back in Augusta, not much of it good. She could be irrational and unpredictable.

But with both of us working, we needed help with daycare for Willem. I mentioned as much during a phone call to my mother one day. "Let me take care of Willem," she said. "I would love it, Emi! It would give me something to do." The idea sounded wonderful to me. I had spent far too little time with my parents since I'd left Istanbul. I procured a military dependent I.D. for my mother and flew her to Germany and she began living with us. Soon, my father, who had since retired from his job at the hospital and then a part-time postal job, came to live with us as well. I loved having my parents around. It was great to spend time with them and do different things with them. We were about an hour from the French border and we'd often visit France on weekends for shopping and dinner.

One Sunday, I took a long walk with my mother. She had now seen my life. She had seen my home and my office. I was a doctor and an officer in the United States Army. We were living well. I had traveled to America and become a citizen of the U.S. as well as a success.

"I can see why you couldn't stay in Turkey, Emi," she said. "You could never have done all this there. I think maybe you were born into the wrong family."

I thought back to when I was growing up and the things I had often said to my mother, about how I didn't want to end up serving a man. I was telling her, in essence, that I didn't want to end up like her. But I realized that my mother had never been offended by this. Though she understood her place in the world, she never allowed that to dictate my place. She wanted more for me. She knew I hadn't belonged in Turkey and, although it meant being separated from me, she knew my move to the States was the best thing that could have happened to me.

"No, Mom," I said. "I wasn't born into the wrong family. I could not have done any of this without you. Don't you remember? The talk we had when I was failing in school? Back in fifth grade you told me I could make something of my life. You and Dad allowed me the independence that I needed to flourish. You allowed the freedom. No, I wasn't born into the wrong family. Far from it. It's because of you that I'm here."

My mother smiled, proud of the daughter she had raised, happy that I had become the woman she was never allowed the chance to become.

Indeed, I had come a long way from Turkey. A long way geographically and a long way across a wide cultural chasm. I had experienced freedom that most Middle Eastern girls dared not dream of. And with freedom comes opportunity. But opportunity does not come freely. With potential for good, there is potential for bad, and if I thought I was on the road to the American dream, I would soon find that the road was not without its potholes and detours.

CHAPTER TEN

Leaving

THE THING ABOUT LIVING a simple life in a simple place, like our village outside of Istanbul, is that you can live a life of relative safety. With limited options come limited risks and with limited risks come limited damage. One can understand the appeal. And I would never begrudge anyone who would choose a life of safety and security. All I can say is that such a life never felt quite right for me. I have always wanted a life of challenges and triumphs, even if the road to triumph came with defeats along the way.

So it was that the freedom of the West appealed to me. But my resolve would be tested, by circumstance and by my own naiveté. Perhaps nowhere was I more naive than in the thorny thicket of love and marriage.

In Germany, I became pregnant again. This time a girl – Cameron, born in 2002. By then, Willem was nearing age three. And yet he wasn't talking. This became a real concern for us. Later we would learn Willem was autistic, but at the time we had no idea what was wrong with him. We just knew he wasn't putting words together. One day I received an email from Scott's mother, a typical message she would send from time to time addressed to nobody in particular and copying in everybody she knew. These emails were always full of updates about what she'd been up to and what was new with the kids. There was a paragraph about Willem. "Willem has still not learned to speak," she wrote. "Of course everybody in the house is speaking Turkey so it's no wonder he can't learn with all that gobbling (no pun intended)."

I was furious. I hit "reply all": "Stephanie, I think the pun was indeed intended. My parents have given up their lives in Turkey to come help us with the children. As for you, you have a nurse taking care of your mother for you because you claim to not have the time. And yet I know you recently returned from Hawaii where you'd spent a month."

Now, Stephanie was furious. She sent me a rambling email full of name-calling and profanities. Then she called Scott and told him to divorce me. "You can't say with that woman," she demanded. When he said he had no plans to leave me, she called him a worthless son. It would be months before the two would talk to each other again.

Scott meanwhile had been pushing me to get out of the Army when my commitment ended. "Let's go somewhere where we can put down roots," he said. "Somewhere quiet where we can raise the kids. I don't want to live a life where we're being asked to move every couple of years, Emi. How am I supposed to get a career started?"

Meanwhile, my career was moving steadily forward. I knew that, in time, I could be a general in the United States Army. Scott knew how I felt about the Army and I knew how he felt about me getting out of the Army. We'd argue about it, and it created a lot of tension around the house even when we weren't arguing about it. It was an issue that wasn't going away. Finally, Scott gave me an ultimatum, threatening divorce. Deep down I understood his position. How could I not understand his desire to pursue a successful career? And I also knew the kids should have their father with them. I didn't want to be divorced, raising kids on my own.

Still, the mood swings were troubling. And my feelings for Scott hadn't been the same ever since the time he'd left me just before Willem was born. Truthfully, I wasn't entirely sure how I felt or what I should do. I talked to my mom about the marriage.

"Emi," she said, "we don't get divorced. Stick it out. You don't want to raise your children without a father. Get him some help for his depression and be patient with him."

I made a deal with Scott. I'd leave the Army if he agreed to seek treatment for his depression. It was the only way. He agreed and we found a doctor in Germany who prescribed medication. The medication helped and Scott soon seemed more like the Scott I had originally met.

I started planning for civilian life. I was licensed to practice endodontics in Alabama, but Scott didn't especially want to go to Alabama. He wanted to be somewhere in the Pacific Northwest, somewhere with hills and mountains. I knew that my license would be good in Oregon, a state that shared reciprocity with Alabama. We agreed on Oregon and rather than start my own endodontics practice, I decided to look for an established one that might be for sale, initially researching the Portland area. Eventually I found a practice for sale in Bend. I did some further research on the demographics of the area and liked what I saw. The city seemed to be a perfect one in which to raise a family. Scott liked the idea of Bend as well.

In the meantime, back in the States, the American Association of Endodontics was having its annual conference. The conference was in Florida and I flew from Germany to attend. After the days' events there were always social activities and on one night there were get-togethers that were hosted by each state. I went to the Oregon get-together and talked to several Oregon endodontists, one of whom was from Bend.

"What do you think of the city?" I asked him. "I'm thinking of buying a practice there and it seems nice."

"Really? Whose practice?"

"His name is Dennis Holt."

"That's me!" he said. The coincidence was remarkable. Dennis told me he was selling because he was retiring and we spent the rest of the evening talking about his practice. He invited me to visit him in Bend and I accepted.

I returned to Germany and then in June of 2003, I flew back to the States, to Bend. I checked out the practice and I checked out the town. I loved it. That year, Bend had been ranked the number one place in the United States to raise children. I wasn't due to get out of the Army until April of the following year, but Dennis suggested I come back in late September of '03.

"I need someone to step in for me for two

weeks," he said. "I'll be on vacation. In Munich for Oktoberfest. Rather than me shut the practice down for those two weeks, why don't you come in and run it? It'll give you a chance to see what it would be like. Kind of a test drive. What do you say?" I thought it was a great idea. So did Scott and in September I went to Bend for two weeks, running the practice and getting a feel for the city. Before I left, I bought us a house. Then it was back to Germany to await the end of my tour.

In the closing weeks, I decided I wanted to go to France once more, specifically to Paris. I had been in a running club with fifteen other girls and there was to be a half-marathon in Paris. We made plans for a weekend trip that would include the race as well as some time to sightsee and shop and visit cafés. My father suggested he'd like to come along.

"I've always wanted to see Paris," he said. "I've never been, you know."

"Maybe another time, Dad," I said. "This is a girl's trip. Do you really want to travel with sixteen girls? We've already made the hotel reservations and we've got a block of eight rooms with two girls to a room. And we'll have the race and everything. I don't think it would be good."

"But, Paris..." he said.

"Leave her alone," my mother told him.

"They've got their plans."

"I'll tell you what, Dad," I said, "Next summer, after I'm settled in Bend for a while, I'll fly back to Paris and I'll send you and Mom a ticket and we'll all meet there. How does that sound?"

"Okay, Emi," he said. "That's what we'll do."

In April of 2004, after my return from Paris, I left the Army. My parents and I said our goodbyes. I thanked them for all of their help. They had enjoyed it immensely and it had been wonderful for the three of us to have spent the time together. We'd become perhaps closer than we'd ever been before.

Scott and I flew to Oregon with Willem and Cameron, and my mother and father returned to Istanbul. We moved into our house and I began working. We were starting a new life. Three months later, I received a phone call. A cousin of mine had gotten married. My parents had attended the wedding and my father had been dancing when suddenly he said he wasn't feeling well. They took him to a doctor who was just about to do an EKG when my father's heart stopped. They tried in vain to resuscitate him. My father died that day. I live with the thought that in his whole life, he never got to see Paris.

CHAPTER ELEVEN

Bend

IT WAS MAY WHEN WE MOVED to Bend and Oregon is beautiful at that time of year. I was excited. It was a brand new chapter in my life. But before long, I started to realize that running an endodontics practice was a lot more work than what I'd experienced as an endodontist in the Army. In the Army, all I had to do was take care of patients as they came in. Now, I was operating a business. That meant not only did I have to take care of patients, I had to make sure I got them in the first place. And I had employees I was suddenly responsible for. And there was paperwork and there were administrative chores.

The practice had already had a good flow of referral business when I bought it, and I did well in keeping the flow going, meeting and courting the referring doctors. But the overhead felt crushing. It was always in the back of my mind. If there were empty spots in my schedule,

I became anxious. In the Army, I'd just wait for the next patient. The pay was the same regardless of the amount of downtime. With my own practice, I thought about the bills that kept coming whether I had any patients or not.

Ironically, the Army had given me more freedom than civilian life. The hours were regular and there were vacation days, thirty of them a year. By the time I had left the Army, I had amassed seventy-two vacation days that I never even got around to using. I never felt especially stressed in the Army, never felt pushed. There was mandatory physical conditioning, of course, but I enjoyed it. I liked keeping myself in shape and always drove myself harder than the Army ever could. It would be the wrong idea to wonder why a girl so committed to freedom would seek the discipline and organizational structure of the U.S. Army. In actuality, in addition to the relative free time, I was given great autonomy. Even my time on duty was mine to schedule as I saw fit, as was the treatment my patients received.

Granted, I was an officer in a medical corps. I never faced combat. I never served on a front line. But even if I had, what the Army provided me with, in retrospect, was nothing less than a future in America. I have often thought back to the days just before I was introduced to the idea of the Reserve Officer Training Corps. I was eating nothing but potatoes and contemplating the idea of ultimately finding my food by scrounging through garbage cans. Even considering shameful ways in which I might earn money to pay rent. The Army saved me.

After the move to Oregon, I was a civilian again, trying to make a go of it with my endodontics practice. It was a stressful period that was made more stressful by Scott. Scott tried looking for a job in Bend but after a few failed attempts, he more or less gave up. He stopped taking his medication as well and he became restless and depressed. I offered him a job in my office and for a time, it worked out well for both of us. Scott was fluent with computers and he was able to set up a management program and train the staff on how to use it. He created the practice website, too, and he jumped in to help answer phones or do whatever else needed to be done. It seemed to give him purpose. Once again, he seemed a little better.

Before long, however, most of Scott's work was completed. Once the computers and software programs and website were set up, there was little for him to do. He was overqualified for answering the phones and setting up appointments. He became bored and restless. Plus, he started to feel more like an employee than a partner in the business. He began to resent the idea of working for his wife and the resentment boiled over. We both maintained a professional civility in the office, but we'd often fight at home.

I now had two children to take care of, plus my husband. There were three employees I felt responsible for. There were office expenses, house payments, payments for daycare, payments for groceries and utilities. Through it all, I felt alone. If Scott resented me, I began to resent him. I needed strength from a husband. Someone to hold my hand and encourage me and tell me everything was going to be all right. Someone to reassure me that we were on the right path.

And then there was Willem. Before kindergarten, he was diagnosed with what they termed a "developmental delay." I didn't really know what that meant but I hung on to the hopes that my son would grow to be a normal child. Although autism would be the eventual diagnosis, I remained in denial about it for some time. Willem was beautiful to me. He had long, curly, golden hair and bright blue eyes. He could run and play and ride his bike and he seemed fine outside of his delayed speech. Some kids are just slow learners, I told myself. He'll be fine.

By this time, Matthew, the son that I had

had with Dale, was graduating from high school. I went to Holbrook, Nebraska, where Dale had been living, to attend the commencement. Matthew had grown into a handsome, well-adjusted young man. Dale had remarried and I met Matthew's stepmom and the two other siblings that Matthew now had. I cried, happy how everything had worked out for Dale and Matthew.

Dorville and Joanne were there and seemed genuinely glad to see me, and I hugged them and thanked them for the time I knew they had spent with Matthew after I had left. Their influence was clear to see. For some reason it didn't occur to me to thank them for what they had done for me. Looking back, it amazes me that these kind people were willing to take a stranger from another land into their home. What would I have done had they not offered up their home to me? How would I have been able to make it in the United States? Regrettably the moment was lost. Both Dorville and Joanne have since passed away and I never got around to offering my gratitude to them for their life-changing kindness.

In February of 2005, I brought my mother over to stay with us for a few months. She'd been alone since my father had died and I thought that staying with us might be good for her. Plus, she could help out around the house and help with the kids. It was nice having her around but her visit was not without its own share of stress. Having her in our house had worked out perfectly in Germany and I assumed it would be the same in Bend. But of course I hadn't thought about the fact that in Germany, my mother had had my father to occupy her. In Bend, she was alone all day long. If Scott was around, they couldn't really communicate with each other; my mother spoke very little English and Scott spoke even less Turkish. I never got home until late. I'd be worn out. My mother wanted to spend the evening talking with me and the kids wanted my attention, too. In the summer, my mother went back to Turkey and I felt bad that I couldn't have spent more quality time with her.

One thing Scott and I agreed on was our concern not just for Willem, but for his younger sister Cameron. If something were to ever happen to Scott and me, responsibility for Willem would fall squarely on Cameron and it seemed like too much of a burden for any one person. We began thinking maybe Willem should have another sister or brother. It's an odd reason to have another child, at least by Western standards. But in Turkey and throughout the Middle East, it's just what families did. You never counted on the government to take care of you. There were few safety nets, even community ones. Your community was your family and your family took care of its own, sharing all of the responsibilities with everyone pitching in. In May of 2006, Scott and I had another daughter – Alex.

By then, Scott began spending less and less time in the office, coming in every now and then just to help with patient reports we would send to the referring doctors. He stayed at home mostly, playing computer games. He would take the kids to daycare and maybe go work out, and then just go home. He seemed to have no motivation to do anything more. By necessity, I was spending twelve hours a day at the office. Working was the only thing that helped me deal with the stress; as long as I was working, the business was moving forward. If I just kept seeing patients, we'd be okay. Eventually, I had to hire a nanny for the kids. And a lawn service and someone to come in to clean the house. Scott did nothing.

His depression kept getting worse and not long after Alex was born, he finally agreed to go see somebody and get back on medication, the original deal that I had made with him in Germany when he'd wanted me to quit the Army. The medication helped. Not long after that, I saw an ad for part-time helicopter pilots. They were needed for battling wildfires of which there were several in the Pacific Northwest that year. I suggested to Scott that he apply to helicopter school. Part-time work would be good for him, especially work that would take him out of the confines of an office environment. He agreed. Soon, Scott seemed to be feeling a little bit better about himself. The problem, however, was that in order to pass the flight physical, he couldn't have the medication in his system. He had to stop taking it a full month before the physical. Once off the meds, it was difficult to get Scott back on them. In his distorted mental state he would accuse me of using the meds to "control" his mind.

Less than a year after Alex was born, I casually mentioned to some friends one day that, even though I was working out, I didn't seem to be able to drop any weight. If anything, I was gaining. "Maybe you're pregnant," one of them said. I laughed at the idea. I was forty-one. Three children were plenty. Later, I began thinking maybe my friend was right. I stopped on the way home and bought a home pregnancy test. It turned up positive. In August of 2007, Scott and I had another boy – Reinhardt.

The marriage was no better, however, and I began to suspect that the distance that had been growing between Scott and me had to do with more than just the stress I'd been feeling and his depression. There was more than just a distance between us. It was as though all of his attention was elsewhere. I began to wonder if there was somebody else.

"Tell me," I said to him one day. "That's all I would ever ask of you. If you don't want to be married to me anymore, just say so. If you ever find someone you'd rather be with and you're going to cheat on me, just tell me first. Give me that much. Then we can get a divorce and you can do anything you want. I won't stop you. But please don't cheat on me while you're still my husband."

"What are you talking about?" he said. "I would never do anything like that."

One night in November, I worked late at the office. My staff was there as well, cleaning. Scott was to come in later and work on reports. He preferred working late, when nobody was there to distract him. I went home and went to bed and shortly afterwards, Scott left for the office. He came home about midnight. The next morning I went to open the office and I found a note on the door from one of the staff members. *Scott, I set the alarm at 9:15.* Scott should have seen the note and picked it up. He obviously hadn't come in. Where was he until midnight, if not the office?

I confronted him and he made up a story

about getting coffee with a friend.

"Where?" I said. "What's open in Bend, Oregon at that time of night? And what friend? I know all your friends. Scott, I'm not an idiot."

He hung on to his story but in the weeks that followed, two different people I knew mentioned to me that they'd seen Scott with another woman. My suspicions had been correct. In December I filed for divorce. Through everything – through Scott's depression, through his lack of attention to the marriage, through his inability to hold a job or even help around the house – I still loved Scott. Sure, it wasn't as strong a love as when we first knew each other, but it was still love and I would not have divorced him for any of what we'd gone through. But the betrayal went too far. I could put up with anything but the cheating.

Scott tried to talk me out of it. He swore he wasn't seeing her anymore. It was a short-lived flirtation, nothing more. "Lots of marriages have rough patches, Emi," he said. "People work through them. We can, too."

We went to counseling. We did joint counseling as well as individual counseling. Once, when it was just me, the counselor recommended I leave Scott. "If you were my sister," he said, leaning forward and lowering his voice, "I would have

told you never to marry this guy in the first place."
But by February of 2008, I found myself softening
to Scott's pleas and promises. He went back on
his medication. Better still, he enlisted in the
Army Reserve. It was a positive step for him. It
seemed to give him purpose again. Maybe, I
thought, I shouldn't give up on Scott. I called my
attorney and told him to stop the divorce proceedings.

In May, Scott went for Reserve training in
South Carolina. Over the Memorial Day weekend,
I took the opportunity to visit Lory and Sue who
had remained in Birmingham after graduating
from dental school and who both had successful
practices. I brought the kids with me and Scott
came over to see us. I was staying at Lory's house
and while she was at work, I was in the kitchen
making something for Reinhardt. Scott was in
the bedroom and I walked back to ask him something and I could see him on his phone. When he
saw me, he quickly flipped it closed without saying another word.

"Who was that?" I said.

"Oh...just my mother."

"You didn't even say goodbye to her." It was
more of an accusation than a statement and Scott
said nothing. What could he really have said?
The kids and I went back to Bend where I re-filed

for divorce.

Between then and October, when he would finally sign the divorce papers, Scott would come and go, staying mainly in Portland with friends but swinging by Bend every now and then to see the kids, even though he didn't spend much time with them when he'd come. One day he left his cell phone behind and I couldn't resist; I took the opportunity to glance at his emails: close to three-thousand of them from his girlfriend, some complete with nude photos. Most of them were from back in March, after I had decided to give him a second chance, after he had sworn he wasn't seeing her anymore, after we had agreed to work things through.

Just as disturbing, maybe even more so, were the emails from his mother encouraging his affair. "Your girlfriend seems nice," she wrote. "Young and lots of fun! Have a good time! Just lie to Emine, and keep lying till you die!" Had I been cheating, I thought, and had it been my mother, I could be certain she would have come over to hasten the dying part. My mother would have killed me. Maybe not literally, but the shame would be worse.

"Well, I guess I just don't want to be married anymore," Scott admitted in the face of the facts. "I don't want to be a father and have a family. It's not who I am. I just can't do it anymore." He signed the divorce papers from New Jersey where the Reserves had sent him and then he was deployed to Iraq in November. Scott was gone and our marriage was over. He'd be sent back to the States, to a military base on Olympia, Washington, in May of 2009, officially diagnosed with bipolar disorder and manic depression.

By then, I had learned what freedom fully entailed. Life was not a fairy tale; I had not been prepared to navigate the choppy waters of a troubled marriage. I had no frame of reference. In Turkey, arranged marriages were simple constructs. There were assigned roles and clear delineations of responsibility. Marriages were covenants of practicality. Emotion played a limited role, love even less so. These things weren't even discussed. From such simplicity I'd come, and my naiveté made it next to impossible to muster up the proper understanding of something as complex as a marriage presumably based on love. My marriage to Dale had been as a very young woman, no more than a teenager, and I had entered into it as though it was an arrangement not unlike my parent's marriage. But with Scott, the marriage had its roots in romantic love, and I'd had no map to follow. All I could do now, alone, with a time-consuming endodontics practice and four kids, was pick myself up and move forward. A little scarred, a little wiser.

TWELVE

Willem

BACK DURING OUR TIME IN Germany, as crude and insensitive as Scott's mother was with her "gobbling" comment, it did occur to me that Willem was possibly not being exposed to English sufficiently to where he could begin to grasp it. There was, in fact, a lot of Turkish being spoken in the house. And outside of the house there was, naturally, a lot of conversation in German. Friends and neighbors were German, and so were the people in the shops and restaurants, many of whom spoke English, but many of whom did not.

In my mind, this helped explained Willem's relative delay in learning to communicate. It wasn't as if he was unintelligent or had nothing to express. He could point to things he wanted and speak in single words. If he wanted milk, he'd say, "Milk." If he wanted to watch "Teletubbies" on TV, he'd say, "Teletubbies." It was clear to me that he wanted to communicate, and could do so, in his own way. But he rarely put anything into a complete sentence or even a phrase, and if he did try to construct a sentence, it was mostly gibberish. Surely, he'll learn in time, I thought.

But I remained concerned and one day I mentioned it to a friend at the office. "Is it normal, do you think, for a three-and-a-half-year-old to not talk?" I asked.

"Why don't you take him to get evaluated?" she suggested. "There are doctors at Ramstein Air Base that can test him. They can probably tell you how he compares with other kids his age."

It hadn't really occurred to me that help might be available, or even to ask for it. My Turkish upbringing. Never thinking of looking beyond the family for support.

At Ramstein, I explained Willem's speech problems. "He has a lot to say," I told them, "but he just can't seem to bring the words out."

Testing determined that Willem was definitely behind where he should have been for his age. The doctors at Ramstein put him in speech therapy.

After the move to Bend in 2004, we continued the therapy. The developmental delay Willem had been diagnosed with prior to kindergarten was officially termed PDD-NOS: "Pervasive De-

velopmental Disorder Not Otherwise Specified,"
a diagnosis that came under the umbrella of
autism. I remained in denial. So did Scott. But as
Willem got older, I could see other symptoms besides his speech. He was having problems dress-
ing himself and tying his shoes. In first grade, it
was decided he should start in the special education class.

By second grade, Willem was still speaking
in single words, still filling in the blanks with gibberish. I decided maybe we could get better re-
sults if we sent him to a private school. I was certain that, given the right foundation, Willem
could catch up with others his age. He was just a
couple of years behind them, it seemed to me,
and I was sure the gap could be bridged. We just
had to work a little harder with him, take more
time with him. I remembered my own struggles
in school, my daydreaming and lack of focus.

The private school did some testing of its
own and the school representative told me they
wouldn't be taking Willem. "I'm sorry, we just
don't really have the resources for him," she said.
"We don't provide the kind of services he needs,
I'm afraid. He wouldn't be a good fit. You'd be
wise to keep Willem in public school where they
can better provide what he needs."

Listening to the school representative, it hit

me, really for the first time, that Willem's problem ran much deeper than just needing to bridge a gap. The gap was going to widen. There would be no catching up. The talk of resources and services brought it all home to me. Willem was not, and would not be, a normally progressing child. The talk with the representative shook me out of my denial. What *was* the future for Willem? Would he ever even be able to speak? That night I looked in on Willem as he slept, my beautiful son, innocently curled up in his bed. I cried most of the night.

Though the private school wouldn't take Willem, they suggested that I look into the programs at Bend Learning Center, a school specifically for children with learning disabilities. I took their advice and at Bend, Willem was put into intensive speech therapy every day from 3:30 until 5:00 p.m. The rate was a hundred dollars per hour and though it added to my level of stress, I couldn't imagine not paying whatever it might take to help Willem.

By then, of course, Scott was gone and Willem and the other kids missed having a father in their lives. Reinhardt, in particular, kept asking when we were going to get a daddy. At these moments, I found myself feeling anger and resentment towards Scott. How could he have left his children? I'd have people over from time to time for get-togethers and Reinhardt, all of about two years old, would sometimes ask one of the male guests, "Are you my daddy?"

The kids at least had a grandmother, of sorts. My mother remained in Turkey and I would have nothing to do with Scott's mom. But for all these years, I had kept in touch with Arlene, the woman who had rented me an apartment in Hawaii. Eventually she would move to San Antonio and the kids and I would visit her there or she would visit our home, always for Christmas. I was raised a Muslim and Arlene was raised a Jew, but that didn't stop us from celebrating Christmas together. It became a tradition. Arlene was always quick with advice, never telling me exactly what to do, but always listening to me thoughtfully and intelligently analyzing any problem I might have had. The kids loved her and she became a surrogate grandma. She remains so to this day.

In 2010, a couple of years after the divorce, the kids and I moved. I'd heard about equine therapy for children with autism. Horseback riding seems to help with social and emotional development, as well as with cognitive skills. The kids bond with the animals and the riding helps with sensory sensations – spatial orientation and balance. Willem's private tutor at Bend, a woman by the name of Heather, approached me one day. "Emi," she said, "I know a guy who's thinking of selling a small ranch. There are horse stalls there and lots of room to ride. Might be perfect for you and the kids. Want to go see it?"

We visited the ranch on a sunny February day. There was snow on the ground and a dusting of it on the branches of the evergreens. The ranch looked beautiful. Gates opened up onto a long driveway that ran to the spacious house. There was a barn and sixteen horse stalls, and another, smaller, house on the land that was rented out to a man who was a part-time hand on the ranch. There was a loft apartment in the barn, as well, which provided some income from the couple who lived there. There was a large pond on the ranch with a gazebo at the water's edge and an island in the center of the pond with a dock. There was a greenhouse and there were chicken coops and even a tree house. The property, forty acres that abutted heavily wooded, federally protected land, rested at the foot of the iconic Three Sisters Mountains.

The ranch had at one time been the country estate of a man who owned a steel mill in Portland. When he died, his son took over. Until then, the son had been living in Europe, and when he returned, he took a small piece of the ranch and replicated, on a much smaller scale, a particular park that had captivated him in France. The little park was full of a wide variety of flowers. Year-round there was something in bloom.

I bought the ranch and the kids loved it. It was a great move for all of us. Spring came and then summer and the kids swam in the pond, played in the tree house, and ran all around the forty acres of land. And of course they rode. We had three horses. Blondie came to us from a woman who had boarded her there with the previous owner. The horse was for the woman's daughter to ride but the daughter went off to college and the woman let us have the horse. A friend let us have Monte, a well-trained horse that was gentle and perfect for Willem. Cheyenne was owned by the couple who lived in the loft apartment. They had wanted to sell her, but when she fractured her leg, they couldn't find a buyer. I agreed to keep her.

We grew hay on the farm and so had a ready supply of sustenance for the horses. The kids took riding lessons and learned how to care for the horses. Cameron rode the most, mostly on Blondie. Willem rode a lot, too, and the experience helped him. Willem loved animals in general, and the riding, as well as the interaction with the horse, boosted his confidence.

I, of course, had no idea how much work was required to maintain a ranch. The part-time hand was invaluable as I knew very little about horses. I paid him by deducting his hours from the rent he paid for the small house, but the other costs of keeping the place up were steep. It was a lot for a divorced woman with a busy endodontics practice and four children. But the stress was off-set by the natural setting of the property, the serenity of it and the beauty of the mountain backdrop. And Willem seemed to thrive there.

Meanwhile, I took up bodybuilding, something I discovered by accident. I had joined a tennis club in Bend and one day a man came in visiting from the San Francisco Bay area. He mentioned that he owned a Max Muscle Sports Nutrition store and asked if there was one around Bend. It happened there was one close by and I showed him where. It was my first time in a Max Muscle and I bought some promotional items – energy drinks and fish oil supplements – and put my address on the store's email list. I returned to the store from time to time and became acquainted with Victoria, the owner, and her partner Josh. They were very involved in bodybuilding and after talking with them about it, I decided to try it.

Bodybuilding was hard work. The weight-lifting was laborious and there were grueling cardio exercises, not to mention a strict dietary regimen. But I loved the discipline, the structure and the organization. I had missed all that from my Army days. Bodybuilding filled a hole and I dove into it hard. I started in January of 2012 and by May, I was entering competitions. I did well. Competing was fun and gratifying.

Meanwhile, Willem's progress, despite the speech therapy at Bend Learning Center and despite the help the ranch seemed to provide, continued to be sluggish. He was beginning to talk more but I could see his rate of development was still much slower than the rate of other kids his age, meaning that as he got older, he was falling farther and farther behind. It was a pace he could never catch up with. By the fifth grade, he began needing occupational therapy because I noticed he couldn't control his fingers and hands the way other kids could.

By this time, Jason Snow, a fellow endodontist, had come to work at my practice. When the economy had taken a dive and both our businesses slowed down, we had decided to merge our offices. The arrangement alleviated a lot of the financial pressure. And having Dr. Snow aboard also allowed me more time at the ranch with the kids. He'd work Monday through Wednesday and I'd work Wednesday through Friday. As it happened, Dr. Snow had a son with Asperger's syndrome, an autism spectrum disorder like Willem's. Our kids were the same age and by complete coincidence, were in the same fifth grade class. Dr. Snow soon found a special school in North Carolina for his son and he and his family began planning to move there. I started thinking of doing something similar.

At a charter school in sixth grade, Willem continued to struggle and in seventh grade I decided to send him back to public school. Things got worse. Willem reached an age where he became painfully aware that he was different. He knew something was wrong with him, even if he didn't know exactly what. He'd embarrass easily. Sometimes in class, he'd become overwhelmed and shut down, putting his head down on the desk.

At Bend Learning Center, Heather continued to tutor Willem privately, one-on-one. He'd spend half a day in his special education classes and a half a day with Heather. It helped. But then my concern became Willem's social development which was lagging as much as his cognitive development. He had difficulty relating to others, a common problem for kids with autism. Half a day alone with a private teacher was half a day without any interaction with his classmates at school. I was at a loss.

I began to learn all I could about Willem's condition. I attended autism conferences. A lot of what I learned was hopeful. There were many smart, talented, creative people with autism. Mozart was most likely autistic. It's believed Einstein may have been autistic. Tim Burton, Andy Warhol, and Dan Aykroyd were all diagnosed with autism. I learned about Temple Grandin, professor and author who was diagnosed with autism and became a famous autism activist. Claire Danes played her in an HBO movie. These people all went on to lead successful, fulfilling lives. Willem could, too.

The key, it seemed to me, was to get the right kind of help. Special education and private tutoring were good starts, but Willem needed more autism-specific therapies, schools and classes that were devoted just to children with autism-spectrum disorders. The problem was that those kinds of programs weren't available locally. "To be honest," one of the school psychologists confessed to me one day, "people who really want to help their autistic children don't move to Bend, Oregon to find it." It was why Dr. Snow had left for North Carolina.

I decided we'd need to move, too. But to where? One thing I'd learned at an autism conference was that testing was available to best determine Willem's specific needs. That way, we could find a school that would be the right match for him. Bend Learning Center tested him and found several schools that would be good matches. Unfortunately, most of them were boarding schools on the east coast and although I was willing to uproot us to go east, there was no way I could be separated from Willem. Boarding schools were out of the question.

Bend then looked into day schools and found some promising possibilities closer, in California. There was a private school in San Rafael, just north of San Francisco, called Star Academy. Willem and I visited the school a couple of times and it seemed perfect. It struck me as if it was Willem's best chance and I felt real hope for the first time. I put the practice and the ranch up for sale.

Scott got wind of our pending move and filed a motion to stop me. Beginning in 2010, he had been seeing the kids every other weekend. They would visit him in Prineville, where he was living, about an hour away. By then, he had remarried. The man who didn't want to be married anymore, or have a family, would soon have a child with his new wife. But it was clear he resented me; I could only imagine that I reminded him of his failures as a husband and father. The resentment continued to fester and litigation against me became something of a hobby for Scott.

On one occasion he refused to allow Willem to bring his dog during a visit, citing an allergy even though his new wife had two dogs. The dog was enormously helpful for Willem and Willem wouldn't go without him. I kept Willem home while the other kids went. Scott took me to court. I had to hire an attorney as well as a specialist who could prove Willem's need for his dog. The dog, the specialist explained, provided comfort for Willem, especially during those times when I was not around. The dog was therapeutic. The court proceedings took up a whole day and though the judge ruled in my favor, the legal fees totaled fifteen-thousand dollars.

Within a year, the dog died and I bought a heartbroken Willem a new one, which he bonded with immediately. The next time the kids went to spend time with Scott, Scott once again refused the dog, claiming the prior ruling was only relevant for the first dog, not the new one. It was frivolous. Again we went to court. Again I was successful. Again it cost thousands.

With the move to California, I managed to

convince Scott that we should enlist a third party to mediate, to save us both the hassle and expense of going to court. But the mediation got nowhere as Scott refused to budge. With the prospect of court looming, Willem's psychologist warned Scott that no judge would take his side on a matter where Willem's mental health was at stake. "You're better off just making a fair visitation schedule with Emine," the psychologist told him. Scott didn't care. He took me to court anyway. This time the legal fees went into the tens of thousands. Once again my attorney brought in specialists, this time to testify on how important it would be for Willem's progress and well-being to enroll him in the California school. After two days of court proceedings, the judge rendered his decision once again in my favor.

"Son," the judge said to Scott, "you made the choice to separate yourself from your family. The important thing now is the welfare of your son. His very future, it seems to me, is at stake and he needs the best help available to him, wherever that might be."

We were all going to miss the ranch, but the kids began looking at California as an exciting, new adventure. So did I. For me, it seemed like the culmination of a long-awaited childhood dream.

CHAPTER THIRTEEN
The Dream

IN SAN RAFAEL, we rented a house that was close to the water. There was a marina nearby and a beach. But there were rolling hills, too, and the whole area was green and so it looked a little like Oregon; it looked familiar. It was also close to the city of San Francisco, which we would visit. The kids adapted well. I was happy with the move and more relaxed and the kids could sense it.

I found a practice for sale in Santa Rosa. A long-time endodontist was retiring. He hadn't taken on many new patients, however, in several years and it took a little while to build the practice back up. I spent a lot of time meeting other doctors and marketing myself but soon enough I had a steady flow of patients. I hired good people, too. I knew that how the staff makes the patients feel can make all the difference and I looked for people who were friendly and caring.

The only problem was the commute. With

traffic, it could take an hour to get from our house in San Rafael to the office in Santa Rosa. To and from meant two hours a day away from the kids. But then I found out about the Anova schools, private schools just for kids with autism and other learning disabilities. There was one in San Rafael, but there was another one in Santa Rosa. During the summer, they held a summer school and I enrolled Willem to see if it was a good fit. He liked it. And so in July of 2015, I bought a house in Santa Rosa and once again we moved.

While enrolling the other kids in the local schools, I learned about a special education class that was run by the county that utilized the local high school. Willem was now high school age and the class, although geared towards students with learning disabilities, allowed interaction with the other high school students. It was a less restrictive environment than Anova. I hoped the interaction would help with the development of Willem's social skills, which continued to concern me. The class itself had only seven other students in it with one teacher and three teacher aides. The extra attention was valuable. So were the role-play exercises that helped the kids learn how to handle themselves in real-life social situations – what's appropriate to say or do and what's not appropriate. Plus, instead of me driving him to school, Willem took the bus which helped him learn more responsibility and independence, in however small a way.

Willem did great, responding well to the class and to the high school environment, and, after a month, I asked the school if we could take things a little further. Could Willem join some regular high school classes? Art class and P. E., in particular. The school agreed and Willem was able to spend more time with other kids. He made some friends with whom he was able to have lunch in the cafeteria. They invited him to go with them to the homecoming dance and he, in turn, invited them to help him celebrate his birthday.

Today, Willem continues to develop. For my part, I've come to terms with the fact that he will always be living with autism. But that doesn't mean he can't thrive. Recently, Willem gave a speech for Bay Area Autism Awareness Day. Temple Grandin was a guest. "Autism is just one part of who I am," Willem said in his speech. "Everyone should be proud of who they are." At Autism Awareness Day, I was certainly proud of Willem.

In the meantime, I've found programs to help Willem when he turns eighteen and gets out into the real world. There's a regional program that will assist him with life skills like securing employment, finding an apartment, getting around, and other basic things that he'll need help with. And of course he'll have me. He'll always have me.

Meanwhile, Cameron and Alex and Reinhardt continue to do exceptionally well. My kids – all of them – remain my pride and my joy. Cameron is thirteen, tall, athletic, a volleyball player. Alex is ten with beautiful blond wavy hair. She skis (black slopes even) and swims. She's musical, as well. Reinhardt, at nine, shares the athleticism of his sisters. He skis, he plays tennis, he's full of energy and seems to be in constant motion.

With all of my kids, I try to make sure they have the opportunities I never had. Would I have played volleyball as a kid? Would I have gone skiing? Given the chance, probably so. But chances to do such things are not often presented to girls where I come from.

But I am finding my opportunities in life now. I recently opened a second practice an hour north of Santa Rosa, in Ukiah. My goal, as long as I can find the right people, is to keep growing.

"Why do you have to work so hard?" my mother said when I told her about it. "Why do you keep driving yourself?" It was just like years before when I told her I was going to college. "Instead of going to college," she had said, "why don't you just find a husband?" It occurs to me that my mother, given her own background, will most likely never truly understand my motivations. But she's happy for me nevertheless. Maybe that's all that counts.

The last time I visited my mother in Turkey was 2014 for a continuous education course on international traumatology. I needed the CE credit and it gave me an excuse to see her, although I could only stay for a couple of days. Prior to that, my last visit had been in 2012. My sister and brothers were there. It was the first time we'd all been together in over twenty-five years.

It was good to see everybody. It was not so good to see Turkey. The country has come far since the days when I grew up there, but in some ways it was very apparent to me that, culturally, Turkey has lately been sliding backwards. There have been more mosques built in the past few years than schools. Islamic conservatives, especially fundamentalists, are speaking with a louder, more ominous, voice. There have been terrorist acts. In October of 2015, two bombs were detonated outside the central railway station in Ankara, killing more than a hundred people and injuring more than four hundred. It will probably get worse.

I grieve for my home nation. I can't think

of my exit from the country without regarding it as, truly, an escape. It's hard to imagine that young girls in Turkey today, should they remain there, have any more of a chance for self-fulfillment and self-actualization than girls had when I lived there.

And yet I would be reluctant to recommend my path for anybody else. A person's life choices are personal. My sister, for example, remains unfulfilled by her move to the States. America is not a panacea. But it remains a land of opportunity and the American dream, as I have learned, is very much alive. There is nowhere else I can imagine being. You have to want it, though. You have to want what America can offer and this is as true for natural-born citizens as it is for immigrants. Immigrants seem to appreciate the dream more, I have found. There are far too many people today, those who were born and raised here, who seem to take for granted all that America offers, as if the American dream is owed to them.

It takes work and it takes true desire. I credit very little of my success to any natural talent or intelligence. Indeed, to say that my elementary school teacher – the one who held a conference with my mother to inform her of my academic shortcomings – would be stunned by what I've managed to accomplish would be a great understatement. My success came from focusing on my dreams and working hard. And maybe more than anything, getting back up whenever I'd be tripped up by circumstance. For this, too, I have learned, is part of a life lived in freedom. With the freedom to succeed comes the freedom to fail. Those potholes and detours on the road to the American dream. But that also means we have the freedom to try again. And again. Perhaps, more than anything, this is what the American dream symbolizes. The United States, I have learned, is a place of second chances.

For me, there have been challenges – in relationships, in career, in family. Each challenge was a price I paid for freedom. Each price was worth the cost. Each price I would pay again.

There is, of course, much left to do. My kids, my career – I have plenty to keep me busy and plenty still to strive for. But the ride so far has been breathtaking. For a woman from Turkey who, as a young girl, was destined to be joined with a husband that would be chosen for her and whom she would serve as a housewife and mother to his children, with her dreams, whatever they may have been, slowly dying on the vine of her youth – for such a woman, the American dream has been nothing short of a miracle.

– The End –

CPSIA information can be obtained
at www.ICGtesting.com
Printed in the USA
LVOW11*1916040817
543600LV00003B/3/P